Tiny House, Big Rules

Mastering the Legal Maze of Small Living

Nathan Venture, D.

Contents

Introduction

The first thing to understand about tiny-house law is that it usually does not fail in one dramatic way. It fails in a hundred small ones. A project gets stalled because a lot is zoned for one dwelling only. A permit gets bounced because the plans do not show a foundation detail. A homeowner is told the unit is "not a house" for one department, but "too much like a house" for another. That kind of mixed message is frustrating, but it is also normal in this space.

That is why tiny-house rules feel so confusing at first. You are not dealing with one clean rulebook. You are dealing with layers of authority, overlapping definitions, and local officials who may be applying old standards to a very new kind of living arrangement. The phrase "tiny house" sounds simple and friendly. The legal system does not care much about friendly. It cares about category.

In practice, category is everything. Is the structure a dwelling, an accessory dwelling unit, a recreational vehicle, a manufactured home, a temporary structure, or something else entirely? Each label can trigger a different set of rules, and the label may change depending on whether the home is on wheels, on a foundation, connected to utilities, occupied full-time, or placed on a particular parcel of land. Two tiny houses that look almost identical from the outside can be treated very differently by a planning department, a building inspector, a lender, or an insurance company.

This is also why local rules matter so much more than internet trends. A tiny-house design that works beautifully in one county may be a nonstarter in the next town over. A community that advertises itself as "tiny-house friendly" may still have strict size minimums, utility requirements, or occupancy limits once you start reading the actual ordinances. Social media is full of inspiring builds; the legal reality lives in zoning maps, code books, permit applications, and deed restrictions. If you skip that part, you are not saving time. You are just borrowing trouble.

It helps to get comfortable with a basic mindset shift: you are not just building a small home, you are building a legally recognized living arrangement. That means you are not only asking, "Can I fit a bed, kitchen, and bathroom into this space?" You are also asking, "Will this be treated as a dwelling where I want to place it?" "What standards must it meet?" "Who has jurisdiction?" "What proof will I need?" Those questions may sound bureaucratic, but they are the difference between a project that moves forward and one that sits half-finished on a trailer while everyone points at someone else.

Another reason the legal side gets messy is that tiny-house living crosses boundaries that the system likes to keep separate. Housing, transportation, construction, land use, sanitation, and taxation all intersect here. A unit on wheels may raise questions about roadworthiness and vehicle registration. A foundation-built unit may trigger residential code and site-development rules. A property with a septic system may have limits that have nothing to do with the house size and everything to do with wastewater capacity. Even if the house itself is perfectly built, the land may not support the way you want to use it.

So this book will keep returning to a few core habits. Read the rule that actually applies, not the one someone online says should apply. Separate what is written from what is assumed. Pay attention to the agency speaking, because different offices often care about different things. And when a rule seems vague, remember that vagueness is not the same thing as permission. Sometimes it means flexibility. Sometimes it means the official on duty gets to decide how the rule is interpreted that day.

That is not meant to scare you off. It is meant to keep you from getting blindsided. Tiny-house legality is not a mystery only specialists can understand. It is a system, and systems can be learned. Once you know what questions matter, the fog starts to lift. The goal from here is simple: help you see the structure behind the confusion so you can make decisions with your eyes open, your paperwork in order, and a lot less guesswork.

Chapter 1: Why Tiny Houses Run Into Big Legal Problems

Tiny houses tend to look simple from the outside, which is exactly why the legal trouble catches so many people off guard. A small footprint can still trigger a long list of rules, and those rules do not always line up neatly with the way tiny-house fans talk about design, mobility, or freedom. Before you get attached to a floor plan or a piece of land, it helps to understand why the law often treats a tiny house as something more complicated than "just a smaller home." The friction usually starts with definitions, then spreads into the local rules that decide what can be built, where it can sit, and how it can be used.

What makes a tiny house legally different from a small house

A tiny house is legally different from a small house not because of its square footage alone, but because the law cares about a whole package of traits: how it is built, where it sits, whether it can move, and whether officials are willing to treat it as a dwelling. A 900-square-foot cottage and a 350-square-foot tiny home may both feel "small," but they often land in very different legal buckets. One may be an ordinary single-family house under the local code. The other may be treated as an accessory dwelling unit, an RV, a manufactured home, a temporary structure, or even something officials are not quite sure how to classify. That classification matters more than the cozy interior or clever storage.

The first big divider is usually whether the unit is on wheels or on a permanent foundation. A tiny house on wheels often looks like a house, but many jurisdictions do not see it that way. Wheels suggest mobility, and mobility can push the unit into RV or trailer territory, even if it has a kitchen, bathroom, and sleeping loft. Once that happens, the rules can change fast. RVs are commonly regulated as vehicles or recreational units, not as permanent residences, which means they may be allowed in an RV park or for temporary use, but not as a full-time home on a standard residential lot. A foundation-built tiny house, by contrast, is more likely to be treated like a traditional dwelling, but only if it meets the local building code and zoning requirements for a house on that parcel.

Another major difference is whether the structure is considered permanent or temporary. The law often asks questions that tiny-house owners do not always expect: Is it anchored? Is it connected to utilities? Is it intended for year-round occupancy? Is it built to be moved, or is it really meant to stay put? Those details can affect everything from permitting to taxation to insurance. A structure that is portable in theory may still be treated as permanent in practice if it is set on blocks, skirted, tied into sewer and power, and used as a long-term residence. On the other hand, a tiny house built to residential standards can still be rejected as a dwelling if the zoning district does not allow a second home on the lot or if the minimum lot size, setback, or occupancy rules do not fit.

Then there is the issue of code compliance. A "small house" can be legally simple if it fits squarely within the local residential code. A tiny house often complicates that picture because it may rely on features that are unusual in standard housing: lofts instead of full bedrooms, compact stairs, ladder access, composting toilets, propane appliances, or off-grid systems. Each of those features can trigger a different review. Some code officials are comfortable with them, especially if the project is clearly an accessory dwelling unit or a custom small home. Others see them as departures from the ordinary rules and want detailed proof that the design still meets safety standards. In other words, the tiny-house label itself does not create the legal problem, but the design choices commonly associated with tiny living often do.

Zoning is where the difference becomes especially obvious. A small house is usually evaluated as a house: Does this lot allow a dwelling of this type and size? A tiny house may have to answer a more complicated question: Does this district allow a dwelling unit at all, and if so, how many, what kind, and under what conditions? Some areas allow one principal residence and one accessory unit. Others allow only a single detached home. Some rural counties are flexible, while some suburban cities are strict about density and minimum floor area. A tiny house can be perfectly safe and well built and still be illegal on a particular lot simply because the zoning ordinance does not recognize it as a permitted form of housing there.

That is why tiny-house legality is often less about the house and more about the category. If the structure is classified as an RV, it may be legal only in certain parks, campgrounds, or temporary situations. If it is classified as a manufactured home, it may need to meet specific federal or state standards and be placed in an approved location. If it is classified as an accessory dwelling unit, it may need to sit behind a main house, meet setback rules, and stay within a size cap. If it is classified as a single-family residence, it may need to satisfy full residential code requirements like ceiling heights, egress, stairs, insulation, and permanent foundation rules. The same physical structure can trigger very different outcomes depending on which box the local government puts it in.

That is also why two tiny houses that look almost identical can be treated differently. One may be approved because it is built on a foundation, submitted with stamped plans, and placed on a lot where accessory units are allowed. The other may be denied because it has wheels, is intended to be moved later, or is parked on land where no second dwelling is allowed. To the owner, the difference may feel arbitrary. To the regulator, the difference is the legal identity of the structure. Tiny-house owners get into trouble when they assume the size of the home is the main issue. In reality, the legal system is usually asking a different question entirely: not "How small is it?" but "What is it, and where is it allowed to exist?"

Why local rules matter more than national trends

One of the easiest mistakes in tiny-house planning is assuming that if something is popular somewhere, it must be workable everywhere. It is not. A tiny house that gets celebrated in a magazine, approved in one county, or parked legally in a model community can still run straight into a wall in the next town over. That is because tiny-house legality is usually decided at the local level, where the people making the rules are thinking about land use, neighborhood character, road access, sewer capacity, fire safety, and long-term enforcement—not about what is trending online.

National trends matter in the sense that they shape the conversation. They influence design, inspire model codes, and help more officials become familiar with the idea of small living. But they do not automatically change what your city, county, or township allows. A national organization can publish a standard, a state can adopt a code framework, and a builder can advertise a "code-compliant tiny house," but none of that guarantees that your parcel is zoned for it, your utility district will serve it, or your local building department will issue a permit. In tiny-house law, popularity is not permission.

Local governments have the sharpest tools because they control the most immediate questions: What can be built on this lot? How many dwellings are allowed? Does the unit need to be on a foundation? Is a tiny house on wheels treated like a house, an RV, or something in between? Can someone live in it full-time, or only temporarily? Those answers often depend on local zoning ordinances, local amendments to state code, and local enforcement habits. Two places can both say they follow the same state building code and still reach very different results because one allows accessory dwelling units by right, another requires a special permit, and a third simply never wrote a rule that clearly fits tiny living.

That local control is also why tiny-house projects can feel inconsistent or even unfair. A county may approve a tiny house on a foundation as an accessory dwelling unit while a neighboring city rejects the same concept because it interprets “dwelling” differently. One inspector may focus on whether the structure meets safety standards, while another may first ask whether the use itself is allowed on the parcel. One planning office may be open to creative solutions, and another may treat anything unconventional as a problem to be avoided. None of that necessarily means anyone is acting in bad faith. It usually means the rules were written for traditional housing and tiny houses have arrived as a legal square peg.

This is why it is risky to start with national examples and work backward. People often see a tiny house village, a YouTube build, or a state-level reform and assume the same path exists at home. But the real question is not whether tiny houses are accepted somewhere. The real question is whether your exact property, in your exact jurisdiction, with your exact proposed use, fits the local rule set. That means you have to pay attention to the smallest details: whether the lot is inside city limits or in unincorporated county land, whether the unit will be permanently connected to utilities, whether it will be occupied year-round, and whether the local code treats it as a dwelling, an accessory unit, an RV, or a temporary structure.

Local rules matter even more because they often interact. Zoning may say one thing, building code another, and health or utility rules something else entirely. A parcel might be zoned in a way that technically allows a second dwelling, but the septic system may not support the added bedroom count. A building department may be willing to review plans, but the zoning office may never allow the use in the first place. A county may permit a tiny house as a residence, but a neighborhood covenant may forbid it. If you only look at the broad national discussion, you can miss the one rule that actually stops the project.

The good news is that local rules are not random once you learn how to read them. They are usually tied to predictable concerns: density, setbacks, square footage, occupancy, utilities, and whether the structure is meant to stay put. When you understand that, you stop asking, “Are tiny houses legal?” and start asking better questions: “Legal where?” “Under what category?” “For how long?” “With what hookups?” “As the main home or as a secondary one?” Those are the questions that determine whether a tiny house is a real option or just a nice idea on paper.

If you want a project to survive contact with reality, local rules are where you have to live. National trends can open doors, but local law decides whether the door is actually unlocked. The farther you get from general inspiration and the closer you get to a specific address, the more the local rulebook takes over. That is not a flaw in the system so much as the system itself. Tiny-house success usually belongs to the people who respect that early, before they buy land, order materials, or assume that what worked somewhere else will work for them.

The most common mistakes first-time tiny house owners make

The first big mistake is treating tiny-house legality like a shopping problem instead of a land-use problem. People fall in love with a floor plan, pick a builder, maybe even put down a deposit, and only then start asking whether the house can actually go where they want it to go. That order of operations causes a lot of pain. A tiny house can be beautifully built and still be illegal on the lot you chose because the zoning does not allow a second dwelling, the parcel is too small for an accessory unit, or the city does not recognize the unit type you bought. If you start with the house instead of the site, you may end up trying to force a legal fit after the fact, which is usually the most expensive way to learn the rules.

The next common misstep is assuming that "tiny" automatically means "easier." In the legal world, smaller does not always mean simpler. A tiny house on wheels may trigger vehicle rules, RV restrictions, or park regulations. A tiny house on a foundation may trigger full residential code, setback rules, utility requirements, and occupancy standards. First-time owners often hear one reassuring phrase from a seller or online forum and treat it like a blanket approval. But local officials do not care that a house is cute, efficient, or Instagram-famous. They care about classification, use, safety, and whether the project fits the district. If you do not know which legal bucket your tiny house is in, you are basically guessing with real money.

Another classic mistake is trusting internet advice more than local paperwork. Tiny-house groups are full of useful experience, but a story about someone parking a house on wheels in one county says very little about what will happen on your property. Even within the same state, one town may allow an accessory dwelling unit, another may require a minimum square footage, and a third may have a rule that quietly blocks the whole idea. First-time owners sometimes collect opinions from builders, neighbors, forums, and social media, then skip the one source that actually matters: the written rules and the written response from the local office. If it is not in the code, the ordinance, the permit notes, or an email from the authority having jurisdiction, it is not something you can safely build a plan around.

People also underestimate how often "temporary" turns into "permanent" in the eyes of regulators. A tiny house parked "for now" in a backyard, on family land, or on a rural parcel can become a problem the moment someone starts sleeping there regularly, hooking up utilities, or treating it like a residence. Owners sometimes think they can avoid the hard rules by calling the setup temporary, seasonal, guest use, or storage. That may work for a short period in some places, but if the actual use looks like a dwelling, officials may treat it like one. The mistake is not just semantic. Once a project is viewed as occupied housing, a whole new set of requirements can appear, and the longer the unit has been sitting there, the harder it can be to unwind the situation.

First-timers also get burned by ignoring the land itself. They focus on the tiny house and forget to check whether the property can support it. Is there legal road access? Can the lot connect to water, septic, sewer, or electricity in a way the county accepts? Is there enough room for setbacks, parking, fire access, or utility placement? Is the parcel in an unincorporated area, a flood zone, an HOA, or a district with extra constraints? A lot that looks perfect on a map can be a dead end once the practical and legal details show up. Owners who skip this step often discover that the hardest part was never the house at all; it was the land.

Another mistake is assuming that one approval solves everything. A permit for a foundation, a certificate for an RV, a variance for setbacks, or a friendly nod from a planner does not automatically clear the project with every other department. Building, zoning, fire, health, utilities, and code enforcement may each have a say. New owners sometimes get one piece of good news and stop asking questions too early. Then they are surprised when a different office raises a separate issue. Tiny-house projects often fail in the gaps between departments, not because one official is being difficult, but because no one approval covers the whole picture.

Finally, a lot of first-time owners make the emotional mistake of treating pushback as proof that the system is broken rather than proof that they need a better strategy. Tiny-house people are often creative, independent, and ready to challenge old assumptions. Those are useful traits, but they can turn into trouble if they lead to a combative approach too early. If you show up insisting that the rules are unfair, vague, or outdated, you may get less help, not more. A better move is to ask clear questions, gather the exact language that applies, and keep the conversation focused on what the project is, where it will sit, and how it will meet the relevant standards. Enthusiasm is a strength. So is patience. The first-time owners who do best are usually the ones who learn to slow down long enough to let the legal picture come into focus before they build themselves into a corner.

How to think like a regulator without losing your enthusiasm

The fastest way to make progress with tiny-house rules is to stop thinking like a builder for a minute and start thinking like the person on the other side of the counter. Regulators are not usually trying to crush your dream. Most of the time, they are trying to answer a few basic questions: Is this safe? Is this allowed here? Who is responsible if something goes wrong? Once you see that, a lot of the weirdness starts to make sense. A permit reviewer who asks for a foundation detail is not being picky for sport; they are checking whether the structure is permanent enough to qualify as a dwelling and whether it meets the standards tied to that status. A zoning official who keeps asking where the house will sit is not ignoring your design; they are deciding whether the use fits the parcel, the setbacks, the density rules, and the neighborhood category.

That shift in perspective matters because tiny-house people often lead with the wrong facts. We talk about wheels, lofts, solar panels, composting toilets, and minimalist living philosophy. Those things may be important to you, but the official usually wants a different set of details first. Think in terms of classification before style. Is it a house, an ADU, an RV, a manufactured home, a temporary structure, or something else under local law? Is it attached to utilities? Is it on a foundation? Is it intended for full-time occupancy? Can it be moved without major disassembly? Those are the kinds of facts that help a regulator place your project into the right legal bucket. If you cannot answer those questions clearly, the person reviewing your application probably cannot either, and uncertainty tends to get translated into delay.

This is where it helps to adopt a very unromantic habit: read every rule as if someone is looking for the easiest reason to say no. That does not mean officials are hostile. It means the system is built around exceptions, conditions, and definitions, and tiny houses often sit right at the edge of those definitions. If a zoning ordinance allows one single-family dwelling per lot, ask yourself what counts as a dwelling in that town. If a code requires a permanent foundation for a house, ask what the jurisdiction means by permanent. If an accessory dwelling is allowed only behind an existing home, ask whether your lot has the required primary residence already in place. This kind of reading is not pessimistic; it is efficient. It saves you from building a plan around a phrase that sounds promising but collapses when you look at the fine print.

It also helps to separate what you want to build from what the government needs to see. You may care about beauty, mobility, low cost, and independence. The reviewer cares about setbacks, height limits, fire separation, sanitation, access, and whether the structure can be legally occupied. When you prepare a site plan, a permit packet, or even an email question, lead with the facts that answer those concerns. Say where the unit will be placed, how it will be accessed, how waste and water will be handled, what code path you believe applies, and what approvals you think are needed. If you are asking about a tiny house on wheels, do not just say it is "basically a house." Explain whether you want it treated as a dwelling, an accessory unit, or a movable structure. If you are asking about a foundation-built tiny home, show that you understand it may need to meet the same expectations as any other residence, just in a smaller package.

Another useful habit is to expect the regulator to care about precedent. Local officials are not only deciding your case; they are also thinking about what happens when the next person comes in with a similar idea. That is why they may seem cautious even when your project sounds harmless. If they approve your tiny house in a way that creates a loophole, they may worry about opening the door to dozens of other projects they cannot manage under the current rules. So when you talk to them, avoid framing your project as a one-off favor or a special exception you deserve because your intentions are good. Instead, show how your proposal fits within existing categories or how it can be reviewed under an existing process. Officials are much more comfortable saying yes to something that looks administrable than to something that feels improvised.

There is also a subtle but important difference between asking, “Can I do this?” and asking, “What would it take to do this legally?” The first question invites a quick yes-or-no answer, and in tiny-house land that answer is often incomplete or misleading. The second question opens the door to requirements, conditions, and next steps. Maybe the answer is that you need a variance, a special permit, a site plan review, a different foundation design, or a different parcel altogether. That may not be the answer you hoped for, but it is far more useful than a vague shrug. A regulator who gives you a process is giving you a path, even if it is not the shortest one.

Thinking like a regulator also means being careful with language. Words such as “portable,” “temporary,” “shed,” “cabin,” “studio,” and “guest house” can mean very different things in different places. If you use the wrong label, you may accidentally send the conversation in the wrong direction. That is why it is smart to describe the physical reality first and let the official tell you the legal category. You do not need to win the vocabulary contest. You need a clear, honest record of what the structure is, where it will be, and how it will be used. Enthusiasm is still welcome. It just works better when it is paired with a little bureaucratic discipline.

Chapter 2: The Legal Map of Tiny Living

Before you can figure out whether a tiny house is allowed, you have to know which rulebook is actually in charge, because the answer is not always the same from one property to the next. A lot of people assume "the law" is one neat stack of rules, but tiny living usually sits inside a tangle of overlapping authority, and that tangle is exactly where confusion starts. One office may care about land use, another about construction standards, another about private restrictions tied to the property itself, and they do not always speak the same language.

Federal, state, county, and city authority explained

In tiny-house law, authority is layered. The federal government sits at the top of the stack, but that does not mean it controls every detail of where you can place a tiny house or how big your loft can be. Most day-to-day decisions happen much closer to home. The trick is knowing which level of government is actually speaking on the issue you care about, because the answer changes depending on whether you are talking about transportation, construction, land use, sanitation, or occupancy.

Federal rules usually matter when your tiny house crosses state lines, connects to national safety standards, or involves a system that is regulated nationwide. If your tiny house is built on a trailer and towed on public roads, federal transportation rules can come into play through vehicle and road-safety standards. If a product inside the house is being sold as part of the build, federal consumer and manufacturing rules may also matter. But the federal government generally does not tell a county whether a tiny house can be used as a primary residence on a specific lot. That kind of decision is usually left to lower levels of government.

State government often acts like the middle layer that connects broad policy to local enforcement. States may adopt building codes, plumbing codes, electrical codes, and fire codes, then let local agencies enforce them. In some places, the state sets the baseline and cities can be stricter. In other places, the state preempts local rules in certain areas and limits how much a county or city can deviate. That is why two tiny houses built to the same plan can face different treatment depending on the state. One state may have a clear path for accessory dwelling units or manufactured housing, while another leaves the issue murky or heavily local.

Counties usually matter most in unincorporated areas, where there is no city government handling zoning and permits. If you buy land outside city limits, the county may be the main authority for land use, septic approval, driveway access, and sometimes building permits. Counties can be surprisingly important in rural tiny-house planning because they often control the practical stuff that makes a dwelling livable: where wastewater goes, how a road connects to the parcel, whether the land is served by utilities, and whether the lot can support another residence. In some places, county rules are straightforward. In others, they are just as strict as city rules, only less familiar to first-time buyers.

City government is where tiny-house dreams often hit the most immediate resistance. Cities tend to have the most detailed zoning ordinances, the most neighborhood pressure, and the most specific rules about minimum lot size, setbacks, density, parking, and the number of dwelling units allowed on a parcel. A city planning department may be less concerned with whether your tiny house is charming and more concerned with whether it counts as a dwelling, an accessory structure, an RV, or something else entirely. If the city does not recognize your chosen category, the project can stall even when the house itself is beautifully built. City officials usually care about whether the use fits the zoning district, whether the structure meets the local code, and whether the project changes the character of the lot in a way the ordinance does not allow.

This is where people get tripped up: the same tiny house can be legal under one authority and blocked by another. A unit might meet state construction standards but still fail a city zoning rule. It might satisfy a county building inspector but not qualify for a full-time occupancy permit because the local land-use code does not allow a second dwelling. Or a tiny house on wheels may be acceptable as a temporary structure under one department, while another department refuses to treat it as a residence at all. That is not necessarily a contradiction. It often means each office is answering a different question. One is asking, “Is it built safely?” Another is asking, “Is it allowed on this lot?” Another is asking, “Can someone legally live here full time?”

Another complication is that authority can overlap without lining up neatly. A state may adopt a building code, but a city may still require permits and inspections. A county may approve septic, but the city may still deny the dwelling use. A federal rule may affect the trailer under your tiny house, but that does not make the house legal to occupy on a residential lot. For tiny-house owners, the practical lesson is that approval from one office is not the same as full legal permission. You want the whole chain to make sense: the structure, the site, the use, and the occupancy all need to survive scrutiny at the level that controls them.

It also helps to remember that “authority” is not just about power; it is about scope. Federal agencies usually regulate national safety and commerce concerns. States often set the framework for codes and licensing. Counties and cities usually control land use and local enforcement. Once you see that split, the process becomes less mysterious. Instead of asking, "Who can make this legal?" ask, "Which level controls this part of the project?" That question leads you to the right office faster, and it keeps you from getting stuck in the all-too-common loop of being sent from one department to another while everybody insists the answer is somewhere else.

Zoning laws versus building codes versus housing standards

Zoning laws, building codes, and housing standards get lumped together all the time, but they do different jobs. If you mix them up, you can end up solving the wrong problem. Zoning is about where a tiny house can go and what kind of use the land is allowed to have. Building codes are about how the structure is built and whether it is safe enough to occupy. Housing standards sit somewhere in between, depending on the state or local program, and usually focus on whether a dwelling meets minimum conditions for human living. A tiny house might satisfy one of these categories and fail another, which is why a project can look perfectly reasonable to the owner and still run into a wall with the local government.

Zoning is the first gate most people hit. It answers questions like: Can this parcel have one home, two homes, or only certain accessory structures? Is a tiny house on wheels treated like a dwelling, an accessory unit, an RV, or something else entirely? Is the lot big enough for what you want to do? Zoning ordinances are usually written to control land use, density, setbacks, lot coverage, parking, and neighborhood character. That means a tiny house can be blocked even if it is beautifully built, because the problem is not the house itself but the fact that the property is not zoned for that use. In many places, a tiny house on a foundation may be treated more like a conventional home, while a tiny house on wheels may be treated more like a vehicle or temporary unit. Same footprint, very different legal outcome.

Building codes answer a different set of questions. They are concerned with structural safety, fire safety, sanitation, emergency escape, stairs, loft access, ceiling height, insulation, electrical work, plumbing, and similar issues. A code official is usually not asking whether your neighborhood likes the look of a tiny house. They are asking whether someone can safely live in it. That is why a tiny house can be allowed by zoning but still fail code review, especially if the design uses steep ladders, low ceilings, unusual lofts, or nonstandard systems. The code does not care that the design is charming or efficient. It cares whether the building meets the minimum requirements adopted in that jurisdiction.

Housing standards are the least familiar category for many tiny-house buyers, but they can matter a lot. These standards often show up in state housing programs, local health and safety rules, landlord-tenant rules, or requirements tied to occupancy permits and habitability. They may not be a full building code, and they may not be a zoning ordinance either, but they can still decide whether a unit can legally be lived in. For example, a local government may have a habitability standard that requires permanent heat, safe sanitation, adequate ventilation, or a certain level of weather protection. In some places, the standards are used to judge whether a dwelling is fit for occupancy after construction or before a rental can be approved. So even if zoning says “yes” and the building code says “close enough,” housing standards can still create a problem if the unit does not meet minimum living conditions.

The important thing is that these three systems do not always line up neatly. A parcel might be zoned for residential use, but the local code may require a minimum dwelling size that your tiny house does not meet. Or a tiny house might meet the state building code as a dwelling, but the zoning department may not allow a second residence on the lot. Or the structure might be allowed as an accessory unit, yet the housing standard for occupancy could require a utility connection or a permanent foundation that your current setup does not have. This is why tiny-house projects get stuck in frustrating loops: one office says the issue is not theirs, while another office says you do not qualify because the first office has not approved the use.

A good way to think about it is to imagine three separate questions being asked at once. First: Is this land allowed to host this kind of thing? That is zoning. Second: Is the structure built safely and to the required standard? That is building code. Third: Is it fit for someone to live in? That is housing standards or habitability rules. If you can answer all three clearly, you are in much better shape. If you can answer only one, you are not done yet. Tiny-house owners often focus on the most visible part of the project—the house itself—when the real legal success depends on the relationship between the house, the lot, and the intended use.

This distinction also explains why asking the right office matters so much. If you call the zoning department with a question about stair dimensions, you may get a vague answer or be sent elsewhere. If you ask the building department whether your lot can host an accessory dwelling unit, you may get told that land use is not their issue. And if you ask a housing inspector whether your tiny house is "legal," you may get a response that depends on whether they are thinking about code compliance, occupancy, or rental habitability. The words may sound interchangeable in everyday speech, but in government they are not. For a tiny-house project, that difference is not academic—it is the difference between a permit path and a dead end.

That is why the smartest tiny-house plans usually start by separating the questions before trying to solve them. Find out what the zoning allows on the property. Then find out what construction standard applies to the structure you want to build or place there. Then check whether any separate housing or occupancy rules apply once someone actually moves in. When you keep those categories straight, the rules stop feeling like one giant blur and start looking like a sequence. Tiny-house legality is hard enough without using the wrong rulebook for the wrong problem.

How homeowners associations and deed restrictions can override your plans

Even if the city says yes, the county is fine with your septic plan, and the building department likes your foundation details, you can still get stopped cold by private rules tied to the property itself. That is the part a lot of tiny-house buyers miss. Public law comes from governments. Private restrictions come from deeds, covenants, homeowners associations, and similar agreements that can run with the land. If you buy into a neighborhood with those rules, you are not just buying dirt and a structure. You are buying into a private rulebook, and that rulebook can be stricter than the local zoning code.

Homeowners associations, or HOAs, are usually created by a recorded declaration or set of covenants that applies to all lots in a subdivision or planned community. Those documents can control things like minimum house size, exterior materials, roof pitch, parking, setbacks, fencing, and where you can store vehicles or equipment. Some of them are written in broad, old-school language that was never meant to contemplate a 250-square-foot home. If the declaration says "single-family dwelling of not less than 1,200 square feet," your tiny house may be a nonstarter even if the town would otherwise permit it. If the rules require a site-built home on a permanent foundation with a certain architectural style, a tiny house on wheels will usually have an even harder time.

Deed restrictions can be just as powerful, and sometimes more annoying because they are easy to overlook. A deed restriction may be recorded against the property itself, or it may be buried in a chain of title, subdivision plat, or separate covenant document. Unlike a zoning map, which you can often check with the local planning office, these restrictions can take more digging to uncover. And because they are private agreements, the people enforcing them are not necessarily government officials. It might be an HOA board, a neighboring owner with enforcement rights, or a developer's successor. That means the fight over your tiny house can become a private dispute even when the government has already given you a permit.

The biggest trap is assuming that "allowed by zoning" means "allowed everywhere." Zoning answers whether the local government will let a use happen. Private restrictions answer whether the neighborhood, subdivision, or recorded documents will tolerate it. You need both. A lot of tiny-house plans die in places that are technically zoned residential but also subject to a covenant saying every home must be at least a certain size. Others get blocked because the HOA bans accessory structures from being used as dwellings, or because the rules require all homes to be connected to the grid in a way your off-grid setup does not satisfy. Even a tiny house that looks tasteful and permanent can still violate a rule written around conventional suburban construction.

It also matters that HOAs and deed restrictions are often enforced through nuisance-level pressure long before anyone files a lawsuit. You might get a warning letter, a fine, a demand to cure the violation, or a threat to place a lien on the property, depending on the governing documents and state law. In some communities, the board has a lot of discretion; in others, enforcement is more limited but still expensive to challenge. And unlike a zoning denial, which may come with a formal appeal path, private enforcement can feel murkier and more personal. That does not make it less real. It just means the process may be less predictable and more emotionally draining.

For tiny-house planning, the key documents are usually the declaration of covenants, conditions, and restrictions; the HOA bylaws and rules; the subdivision plat; and the deed itself. Read the actual language, not just the marketing brochure for the neighborhood. Watch for phrases like "minimum dwelling size," "permanent residence," "approved architectural style," "no temporary structures," "no trailers," "no recreational vehicles," and "no outbuildings used as living quarters." Those phrases can do a lot of work. Sometimes the rule is obvious. Other times it is hidden in a definition. For example, a document may define a "dwelling" in a way that quietly excludes a unit on wheels, or it may require that all homes be "constructed on site," which can create problems for factory-built tiny houses as well.

There are a few situations where private restrictions and tiny-house goals can still line up, but you have to verify it before you commit. Some newer communities have more flexible design standards. Some HOAs allow accessory dwelling units if they meet appearance and utility requirements. Some rural properties are not part of any association at all, which removes one layer of trouble, though not the public rules. But if you are relying on a variance, a board exception, or a friendly conversation with one committee member, treat that as fragile until it is in writing and authorized under the governing documents. A verbal "that should be fine" is not much protection when the board changes, neighbors complain, or the property is sold.

The safest move is to check private restrictions before you buy land, before you sign a build contract, and before you assume a permit solves the whole problem. If the documents are unclear, get them reviewed by someone who can read real estate restrictions for a living. In tiny-house projects, the legal fight is often not about whether the structure is beautiful, safe, or even code-compliant. It is about whether the property came with private promises that quietly say, "not here."

Where to find the rules that actually apply to your property

The first place to look is always the property itself. That sounds obvious, but tiny-house projects go sideways when people start with internet advice, a builder's sales pitch, or a friend's success story in another town. The rules that matter are the ones tied to your exact parcel, not the ones that sound close enough. A lot of tiny-house legality comes down to three questions: what the land is zoned for, what private restrictions burden the land, and what departments have authority over how a home can be placed there. If you do not answer those three questions early, you are basically planning in the dark.

Start with the local planning or zoning department and ask for the zoning designation of the parcel. You want the exact map classification, not just a general neighborhood name. A property might be in a residential district, agricultural district, rural district, mixed-use district, or something more specialized, and each one can treat tiny houses differently. Once you know the zoning label, ask for the written rules that apply to that district: permitted uses, minimum lot size, setbacks, density limits, accessory dwelling unit rules, and any special standards for dwellings on wheels or small dwellings. If the office has a zoning map online, print or save the page. If it does not, ask for a copy. The goal is to build a paper trail, not rely on memory from a phone call.

Next, check whether the property sits inside city limits, in unincorporated county land, or in a special district. That distinction matters more than many first-time buyers realize. A parcel just outside a city boundary may be subject to a completely different set of rules, even if it looks like the same neighborhood from the road. Counties often handle land use differently than cities, and unincorporated areas may have fewer services but also fewer assumptions about standard suburban housing. If the parcel is in a subdivision, planned community, or HOA-controlled area, get the private rules too. A county planner can tell you what the county allows, but they cannot override a deed restriction or HOA covenant. You need both pictures at once.

Then move from zoning to building and health-related departments. A lot of tiny-house buyers stop after zoning because the answer there sounds promising, only to discover that the building department, fire marshal, health department, or utility provider has its own requirements. Ask which department reviews the structure type you are considering. If it is a tiny house on wheels, ask whether it is treated as an RV, a manufactured dwelling, or something else for local enforcement purposes. If it is on a foundation, ask whether it must meet the full residential code or a smaller dwelling standard. If you plan to use well water, septic, composting toilets, off-grid power, or another nonstandard system, those approvals may come from different offices entirely. One office saying “maybe” is not the same as getting all the needed yeses.

It also helps to ask the question in a way that forces specificity. “Can I put a tiny house here?” is too vague to be useful, because the answer depends on size, foundation, occupancy, utilities, and whether the unit is primary housing, a guest house, an ADU, or temporary lodging. A better approach is to describe the exact legal setup you want: “This parcel is zoned X. I want to place a 320-square-foot dwelling on a permanent foundation as a secondary unit behind an existing single-family home. What permits, approvals, and code standards apply?” If you are buying land, ask before closing whether the lot can support the intended use. If you already own it, ask before ordering plans. Tiny-house law punishes assumptions and rewards precision.

Don't forget the boring documents, because they often contain the real answer. The zoning ordinance, land development code, subdivision plat, deed, title report, and HOA documents can all matter. Sometimes the key detail is buried in a definition section, where the code distinguishes between a "dwelling," a "manufactured home," a "recreational vehicle," and an "accessory structure." Sometimes the decisive rule is not a ban but a size threshold, a minimum width, or a requirement that a dwelling be attached to a foundation. Sometimes the land can support one house but not two, or a house but not an accessory unit. Reading the actual text may feel slow, but it prevents the classic tiny-house mistake of relying on someone else's shorthand version of the rules.

If you want to be efficient, make yourself a simple property file and keep every answer in writing. Include the parcel number, zoning designation, map screenshots, relevant ordinance sections, email responses from officials, and any notes from phone calls with dates and names. When you ask a question, ask who reviewed it and whether they are speaking generally or about your specific parcel. If the answer is verbal, follow up by email: "Thanks for speaking with me today. My understanding is that the parcel at [address] is zoned [district], and that [summary of answer]. Please let me know if I misunderstood anything." That kind of record does two things at once: it helps you stay organized, and it makes it much easier to spot contradictions before they turn into expensive mistakes.

The last thing to check is whether the property has hidden limits that are not obvious from a quick map search. Easements can affect where a tiny house can sit. Floodplain, wildfire, coastal, historic, or environmental overlays can add extra layers of review. Road access can matter if emergency vehicles need to reach the site. Utility availability can matter if the land is technically buildable but not realistically serviceable. Even a parcel that looks perfect on paper may have one deal-breaking constraint tucked inside a separate map, report, or recorded document. The property is not just a dot on a zoning map; it is a stack of rules attached to one specific piece of land. Your job is to uncover that stack before you commit to the dream.

Chapter 3: Zoning Laws Made Simple

Zoning is where tiny-house plans usually hit their first real wall, because this is the part of the legal process that decides what a piece of land is supposed to be used for in the first place. Before anyone worries about floor plans, loft ladders, or finishes, the local zoning code is already asking a bigger question: does this property allow the kind of living arrangement you want? That answer can change a lot depending on whether the land is residential, agricultural, rural, or mixed-use, and it can change again depending on whether your tiny house is on wheels, on a foundation, or intended to function as an accessory dwelling.

Residential, agricultural, rural, and mixed-use zoning basics

Residential zoning is usually the first place tiny-house dreams run into hard limits, because it is built around a very ordinary assumption: a residential lot is meant to hold a conventional home, and maybe a few closely related uses, not a menu of housing experiments. In a lot of places, the code will not say "tiny houses are banned." It will say something more boring and more effective, like one dwelling unit per lot, a minimum house size, or a requirement that a dwelling be built on a permanent foundation. Those rules can shut the door on a tiny house even when the structure itself is safe and well built. The key question in residential zoning is not “Is this cute and livable?” It is “Does this count as the kind of residence this district allows?”

That is why the exact wording matters so much. A district that allows “single-family detached dwellings” may sound friendly, but if the code defines a dwelling in a way that excludes units on wheels, accessory structures, or anything without a permanent foundation, the phrase stops being helpful. Some residential zones are also very picky about lot coverage, setbacks, height, and minimum floor area. A tiny house can be too small to violate a minimum size rule and still fail because the zoning code expects a primary residence to meet a certain standard of permanence or appearance. In other words, you are not just checking whether a house can physically fit on the lot. You are checking whether the district recognizes that kind of house as a permitted residential use.

Agricultural zoning can feel more flexible, and sometimes it is, but it is not a free pass. People often hear “ag land” and assume they can place almost anything there because the land is rural and open. Sometimes that is partly true, especially where the code is written to preserve farming, allow farmworker housing, or support low-density rural living. But agricultural districts often come with their own limits. They may allow a farmhouse, a second dwelling for family or workers, or a temporary structure tied to active farm operations, while still restricting the kind of year-round independent living a tiny house owner wants. Some counties treat agricultural land as a place for production first and housing second, so a tiny house can be allowed only if it is clearly connected to the agricultural use or paired with a qualifying residence.

The real trap in agricultural zones is assuming that low population density means low regulation. It does not. You may get more room to breathe on setbacks, lot size, or secondary dwellings, but you may also face stricter expectations about access, water, septic capacity, and whether the land is actually being used for agriculture in a meaningful way. If the parcel is just "rural-looking" but not truly agricultural under the code, the zoning office may treat it like any other lot. And if the district allows farm-related housing but not ordinary residential subdivision-style development, a tiny house marketed as a full-time home can still be denied. Agricultural zoning can be friendly to tiny living, but only when your use matches the district's purpose.

Rural zoning sits somewhere in the middle and is often the most misunderstood. Rural districts are usually designed for lower density, larger parcels, and a mix of uses that would not fit neatly in a suburban subdivision. That can make them promising for tiny houses, especially foundation-built homes or accessory units on larger tracts. But "rural" does not automatically mean "anything goes." Some rural zones still require a minimum dwelling size, a permanent foundation, or a primary residence before any second unit is allowed. Others allow mobile or temporary units only during construction or for limited occupancy. A lot of tiny-house buyers mistake rural character for legal flexibility, then discover the code still cares a great deal about whether the structure is a dwelling, an accessory structure, or a temporary shelter.

Mixed-use zoning is a different animal altogether. These districts are usually created to blend housing, retail, offices, and sometimes light industrial or community uses. That can make them surprisingly useful for tiny-house projects, especially if the plan involves live-work arrangements, courtyard housing, or a small dwelling above or behind a business. The upside is that mixed-use districts often think in terms of compatibility rather than strict one-size-fits-all residential uniformity. The downside is that they may be even more specific about what type of housing is allowed, how the dwelling relates to the nonresidential use, and whether the unit is part of a larger approved development. A tiny house in a mixed-use zone may be easier to approve if it supports a business or fits a planned development, but harder if you are trying to use a standalone lot in a way the district did not anticipate.

The smartest way to read these zones is to look for the hidden assumptions. Ask whether the district allows one dwelling or multiple dwellings. Ask whether the dwelling must be on a foundation. Ask whether accessory dwelling units are allowed, and if so, whether they must be attached, detached, owner-occupied, or limited by size. Ask whether temporary occupancy is allowed at all. And do not stop at the use table. Definitions, dimensional standards, and notes at the end of the ordinance often carry the real rules. A tiny house project can look allowed in one section and get quietly disqualified in another.

If you are comparing residential, agricultural, rural, and mixed-use land, the practical difference is not just how the lots look. It is how the local government imagines people living on them. Residential zoning usually wants predictability and conformity. Agricultural zoning usually wants land tied to productive use. Rural zoning usually wants low density and flexibility, but not necessarily novelty. Mixed-use zoning usually wants compatibility and efficiency. Tiny houses can fit into all four, but rarely by accident. They fit when the project is framed in the language the district already understands, and when the parcel's zoning actually leaves room for the kind of home you want to build.

Tiny houses on wheels versus tiny houses on foundations

The legal split between a tiny house on wheels and a tiny house on a foundation is bigger than most people expect, because the law is not just looking at size. It is looking at the structure's identity. A tiny house on wheels often gets treated more like a vehicle, trailer, or recreational unit, while a tiny house on a foundation is usually treated like a dwelling or a permanent building. That difference affects almost everything that comes next: where it can sit, what permits it needs, whether it has to meet residential code, and which office gets to decide its fate.

A tiny house on wheels can sound appealing because it feels flexible. You can move it, park it, and in some cases avoid the same construction rules that apply to a conventional house. But that mobility is also why local officials may hesitate to recognize it as a legal home. If the unit still has wheels, a hitch, and a trailer frame, a zoning officer may decide it is not a permanent dwelling at all. It might be allowed only in places where RVs, temporary lodging, or accessory uses are permitted. In some jurisdictions, that means it can be stored on a lot but not occupied as a residence. In others, it may need to stay in a designated park or campground rather than a standard residential neighborhood.

That is why the question “Can I live in it?” is not the same as “Can I own it?” or even “Can I park it on my land?” A tiny house on wheels may pass inspection as a road-legal trailer, but still fail as a legal residence. It may be built to RV standards, but those standards are not the same as the local building code for a house. Some places are comfortable with this and create a path for tiny homes on wheels through RV parks, tiny-house communities, or special zoning categories. Others draw a hard line and say that if it is on wheels, it is not a house for year-round occupancy. That is a legal classification issue, not a design issue.

A tiny house on a foundation usually follows a different track because the foundation signals permanence. Once the structure is anchored to land, the local government is more likely to treat it as a building subject to residential code, setback rules, lot coverage limits, utility requirements, and occupancy standards. That can be a good thing, because it may open the door to legal year-round living in places where a wheeled unit would never be accepted. It can also be a headache, because the minute you move into permanent-building territory, you may have to meet minimum ceiling heights, stair requirements, insulation standards, frost-depth footing rules, and all the other details that come with a real house.

The foundation route often gives you more legal stability, but it also reduces flexibility. You cannot simply hook up and leave if the zoning changes or the neighbors complain. You are tied to the parcel, which means the land itself has to support the project. That includes not just zoning, but also setbacks, minimum lot size, septic capacity, driveway access, and sometimes utility availability. A foundation-built tiny house may be perfectly legal in one rural county and completely impossible in a dense suburb, even if the floor plan is identical. The house is not the only thing being regulated; the land and its intended use matter just as much.

Wheels versus foundation also affects how local departments talk about the project. With a wheeled unit, you may be dealing with a planning department, a parks office, an RV code, or a transportation-related classification. With a foundation home, you are more likely to be dealing with building officials, inspectors, and zoning staff who expect a permanent residence. That difference matters because each office asks different questions. One wants to know whether the unit can be towed safely. Another wants to know whether the structure can withstand wind, snow, and seismic loads. If you bring the wrong assumptions to the wrong office, you can get a vague answer that sounds like approval but is really just a polite deflection.

For tiny-house buyers, the practical takeaway is that the build style should match the legal path, not the other way around. If you want the freedom of a wheeled unit, you need to find out where that kind of unit is allowed to be occupied, not just stored. If you want the permanence of a foundation home, you need to be ready for the code and zoning obligations that come with it. A lot of tiny-house trouble starts when people build first and classify later. The smarter move is to decide early whether you are aiming for a movable unit or a permanent dwelling, then confirm that the local rules actually support that choice before the first board is cut or the first axle is welded on.

Accessory dwelling units, secondary units, and backyard homes

Accessory dwelling units, secondary units, and backyard homes are one of the friendlier legal pathways for tiny living, but they are not a free pass. In a lot of places, these terms describe a small, secondary home on the same lot as a primary residence. That can be a huge advantage because the law is already set up to think about the property as having more than one living space. Instead of trying to convince a city to treat your tiny house like a brand-new category of housing, you are often working within a framework that already expects an extra unit. That said, the local code may call it an ADU, a secondary suite, a granny flat, a carriage house, a laneway house, or something else entirely, and the label matters less than the rules attached to it.

The first thing to understand is that an ADU is usually tied to an existing main dwelling. That means the lot already has a primary house, and the tiny house is being added as a second place to live. Some jurisdictions allow the secondary unit to be attached to the main house, like a basement apartment or an over-garage unit. Others allow detached units in the backyard. A few allow both. The details can get very specific: maximum square footage, height limits, setbacks from property lines, parking requirements, owner-occupancy rules, and limits on whether the unit can be sold separately from the main house. If your tiny house is meant to be the secondary unit, those details are not side issues. They are the whole game.

Detached backyard homes are especially attractive to tiny-house owners because they seem to match the lifestyle so well. You get privacy, a small footprint, and a separate structure that feels like its own little home. But a backyard home still has to fit the local definition of an accessory unit if you want it approved that way. Some cities care a lot about whether the unit is permanent or movable. Others care more about the foundation, utility connections, and whether the structure looks residential enough to blend with the neighborhood. A tiny house on wheels may be a terrible fit for an ADU program even if the floor plan is perfect, because the city may want a site-built structure with a standard foundation and permanent hookups.

This is where tiny-house owners sometimes get tripped up by the word accessory. It does not mean "small and optional" in the casual sense. It means subordinate to the main residence. That usually affects size, location, and even how the unit is used. A local ordinance may say the accessory unit cannot be larger than a certain percentage of the main home, or it may cap the size at a fixed number of square feet. It may require the unit to be behind the main house rather than in front, or it may limit the number of bedrooms. In some places, the code also limits who can live there, especially if the property is in a single-family district that is trying to preserve a certain density pattern.

Parking is another issue that comes up fast. Some cities require one additional off-street parking space for an ADU, while others have relaxed that rule because parking requirements were making these units impossible to build. If the property is near transit, in a historic district, or in a compact urban area, the parking rule may be waived or reduced. But do not assume that will happen automatically. Tiny-house projects get delayed all the time because the owner assumed the backyard unit would "obviously" count as an accessory dwelling and then discovered the city also wanted a new parking spot, a wider driveway, or proof that the street can handle more cars.

Utilities can be just as important as zoning. A detached backyard home may need separate water, sewer, or electrical connections, or it may be allowed to share services with the main house under certain conditions. In some places, the sewer department has its own rules about capacity and tie-ins, and the water utility may want a separate meter. Septic systems can be especially tricky, because adding a second dwelling may require a bigger system or a fresh capacity review. A lot of people focus on whether the zoning code allows the unit and forget that the utility side of the project can still stop it cold. If the lot cannot support the extra load, the legal permission on paper may not matter much.

There is also a strategic reason tiny-house owners like ADUs: they often offer the cleanest path to legal occupancy. If the city has a real ADU program, you may be able to get a permit, pass inspections, and end up with a recognized dwelling instead of a gray-area structure. That can help with financing, insurance, resale, and long-term stability. But the tradeoff is that you usually give up some flexibility. An ADU is not the same thing as a free-standing tiny house parked wherever you want it. It is part of a regulated property relationship, and the main house, the lot size, and the local ordinance all shape what is possible.

That is why the smartest first question is not "Can I build a tiny house in this backyard?" It is "Does this jurisdiction allow an accessory dwelling unit, and if so, what exact form does it have to take?" Once you know that, you can work backward from the rules instead of trying to force a tiny-house design into a category it does not fit. In some places, that will mean a foundation-built backyard cottage. In others, it may mean a converted garage, an attached addition, or a small detached unit with permanent utilities. The dream is still a tiny home. The legal path just depends on which version of "secondary unit" the local code is willing to recognize.

Common zoning exceptions, variances, and special-use permits

A zoning exception is the broadest kind of relief, and in tiny-house land it usually means the local code already has a rule that does not quite fit your project, but the government has created a way to make an exception in limited cases. That might show up as a special overlay district, a planned unit development, a rural cluster option, or a local ordinance that specifically allows accessory dwelling units, manufactured homes, or small-footprint housing in certain places. The important thing is that an exception is not you asking officials to ignore the rules. It is you using a rule the code already provides. That distinction matters, because if the code has a built-in path, your odds are usually better and the process is often more predictable.

A variance is different. A variance is usually a request to bend a zoning rule because your property has some unique hardship that makes strict compliance unusually difficult. Think of things like an oddly shaped lot, a steep slope, a narrow buildable area, a floodplain edge, or an existing house placement that leaves little room for a second structure. What a variance is not supposed to be is a shortcut just because the project would be easier or cheaper if the rule did not apply. Many zoning boards are cautious about variances for exactly that reason. If the same rule would be inconvenient for lots of people, it is less likely to be seen as a true hardship and more likely to be treated as a general policy issue that should be solved by changing the ordinance, not by granting one-off relief.

Special-use permits, sometimes called conditional-use permits, are another path altogether. These are used when the zoning code says a use may be allowed in a district, but only after extra review and sometimes only if certain conditions are met. This is common in places where the local government is willing to allow something like an ADU, a tiny home park, a guest cottage, a group living arrangement, or a small manufactured home setup, but wants to control details such as traffic, parking, utilities, setbacks, screening, or occupancy. The idea is not "yes or no" so much as "yes, if you can show us this will work here." For tiny-house owners, that can be a useful middle ground when the use is not clearly allowed by right but is not completely off the table either.

The names change from place to place, and that alone can trip people up. One county may call it a variance, another a special exception, another a special permit, and another a use permit. The label is less important than the actual standard. Some approvals are about land use compatibility, some are about physical site constraints, and some are about discretionary judgment by a board or hearing officer. If you are trying to fit a tiny house into a local process, read the code carefully enough to know what the decision-maker is really being asked to decide. A request that sounds technical may actually be political, and a request that sounds flexible may still have a very strict checklist behind it.

For tiny houses, the most common place these tools come into play is when the zoning code is close to allowing what you want, but not quite. Maybe the lot is large enough for a second dwelling, but the code demands a minimum size that your tiny house does not meet. Maybe the district allows an ADU, but only behind a primary home and only if the owner lives on-site. Maybe the parcel is in a rural zone where dwellings are allowed, but the setback rules leave no practical place to put a small structure without encroaching. In those situations, a variance or special permit can sometimes bridge the gap, but only if the facts line up with the local standards. Officials are much more likely to look favorably on a project that solves a genuine site problem than one that simply wants to avoid the ordinary rules.

The application itself usually matters as much as the rule you are asking to bend. A weak request tends to sound like, "I want a tiny house and the code is too restrictive." A stronger request sounds like, "The property has a unique condition, the proposal still meets the purpose of the zoning district, and the impact on neighbors will be minimal." That means bringing site plans, dimensions, setbacks, utility details, parking information, and anything else that helps the board see the real-world picture. If the local process allows public notice or a hearing, be ready for neighbors to ask about noise, privacy, traffic, and property values, even if those concerns are more emotional than technical. The more clearly you show that your project is orderly, safe, and compatible with the neighborhood, the easier it is for the decision-maker to justify approval.

It also helps to know what these tools cannot usually do. A variance will not magically override a state building code, a deed restriction, or an HOA rule. A special-use permit will not necessarily cure a problem with lot size if the ordinance still requires a minimum parcel area that your land does not meet. And an exception built into zoning does not always solve the separate question of whether the structure qualifies as a legal dwelling under building or housing rules. Tiny-house projects often need more than one approval at the same time, and getting one piece of relief does not mean the rest of the path is clear. That is why people get into trouble when they hear "we can probably make an exception" and stop asking questions too early.

The smartest way to approach these options is to treat them like a menu of legal tools, not a wish list. Start by finding out whether the code already has an allowed path for your exact use. If not, ask whether the issue is a variance, a conditional approval, or a broader zoning amendment. Then compare the burden of each route: what evidence is required, who decides, whether there is a public hearing, how long it takes, and whether approval runs with the land or only with the current owner. In tiny-house planning, the right exception can turn a dead end into a workable project. The wrong one can waste months and still leave you with a no.

Chapter 4: Building Codes, Safety Rules, and What Counts as a House

Once a tiny house gets past the question of where it can sit, the next fight is usually about whether it is built in a way the law can accept as a real place to live. That is where building codes and safety rules step in, and they are less about style or personal preference than about whether the structure meets the minimum standard the local authority is willing to recognize. This is also where tiny-house projects tend to get split into different legal tracks, because the same design can be treated very differently depending on how it is constructed and what category officials think it belongs in.

How building codes are written and enforced

Building codes are not usually written by one person sitting in an office and inventing rules from scratch. They are assembled from model codes, state amendments, local tweaks, and a long history of "we learned this the hard way." That is why the code language can feel oddly specific in one place and strangely vague in another. A code may tell you exactly how wide a stair must be, but leave a lot of room for interpretation on whether a sleeping loft ladder counts as a stair. It may define a "dwelling unit" in one section and then use that term casually throughout the rest of the code as if everyone already agrees on what it means. For tiny-house builders, that matters because the code is not just a safety manual. It is a legal document, and the words inside it control what an official can approve, question, or reject.

Most building codes start with a model code published by a national organization, then get adopted by a state or local government with changes. Those changes can be small or huge. One state may accept the model language almost as written. Another may delete certain provisions, add stricter energy rules, or create a special appendix for tiny houses. A city may then layer on its own requirements through local amendments or administrative policies. So when someone says, “The code allows it,” the real question is: which code, in which version, with which amendments? Tiny-house projects often get tripped up because builders assume the code is a single national standard. It is not. It is more like a family of related rulebooks, and the local edition is the one that counts.

The writing style of building codes also explains why they can be so frustrating to read. Codes are designed to be enforceable, not friendly. They use defined terms, exceptions, and cross-references because officials need language that can stand up to challenge. That means a tiny-house owner may have to read three sections to understand one requirement. A rule about loft safety might depend on whether the loft is considered habitable space. A rule about ceiling height might depend on whether the space is a living area, a bathroom, or a storage loft. A rule about emergency escape might depend on the size and location of a window, the height above grade, and whether the room is classified as a bedroom. The code is really a chain of definitions, and if one link does not fit your design, the whole chain can break.

Enforcement is where the written code becomes real. In most places, the building department is the gatekeeper, and the process usually starts with plan review. Before anyone pours concrete or installs framing, a reviewer looks at drawings and checks whether the design appears to meet the code on paper. If the plans are incomplete, unclear, or use a detail the reviewer cannot verify, the permit can be delayed or denied. After that come inspections, where an inspector checks the work at specific stages. Framing, rough plumbing, electrical, insulation, and final occupancy are common checkpoints. The inspector is not there to redesign your house. The job is to compare what was built to what was approved and to the minimum standard in the code. If the approved plans and the actual construction diverge, that can create a problem even if the finished space seems perfectly livable.

This is one reason tiny houses on wheels and tiny houses on foundations can be treated so differently. A code official is not only asking, "Is it safe?" but also, "What category does this belong in?" If the structure is considered a dwelling, the code may expect standard residential features, permanent utilities, and certain dimensions. If it is treated as a trailer or recreational unit, a different set of standards may apply, and the building department may step back entirely or require a different approval path. Tiny-house owners often get in trouble when they try to blur those categories. A unit that looks like a house but sits on a trailer can trigger questions about whether it is actually a dwelling at all. That classification issue is not a side detail. It is often the main event.

Another thing to understand is that codes are enforced through discretion, but not unlimited discretion. Inspectors and plan reviewers usually have some room to interpret ambiguous language, especially when the code does not spell out every tiny-house scenario. That can work in your favor if you present a well-documented project and show that your design meets the intent of the rule. But discretion cuts both ways. If your plans are vague, inconsistent, or obviously trying to squeeze around the code, an official is more likely to take a conservative stance. In tiny-house work, "close enough" is rarely a good strategy. The smaller the structure, the more likely every inch and every detail matters, because there is less room to absorb a missed requirement.

It also helps to remember that enforcement is not always about catching people doing something wrong after the fact. A lot of code enforcement is preventive. The system is built to stop unsafe or noncompliant construction before it becomes an occupied home. That is why officials care so much about drawings, product approvals, engineering letters, and staged inspections. They are trying to reduce the odds of a problem that would be expensive or dangerous to fix later. If you understand that mindset, the process makes more sense. The reviewer asking for more detail is usually not being difficult for sport. They are trying to decide whether your tiny house can be approved under the rules they are required to enforce, and whether the paper trail is strong enough to support that approval.

Minimum ceiling height, loft, stair, and egress requirements

This is the part of the code where a tiny house can go from "cute and clever" to "not approved" very fast. Ceiling height, loft access, stair design, and emergency escape are all places where the law stops caring about your square footage and starts caring about whether a person can actually live there without getting trapped, injured, or squeezed into a space that is too low to be usable. The trouble is that tiny-house design often pushes right up against these limits on purpose. A low ceiling saves room. A loft creates sleeping space. A narrow stair or ladder fits the layout. But once those choices intersect with code language, the details matter a lot more than the overall vibe of the house.

Minimum ceiling height rules usually show up in the main living areas first. Many codes want a certain amount of headroom in habitable rooms, and that makes sense when you think about daily use. A space where people cook, sit, and move around should not feel like a crawlspace. The exact number can vary by jurisdiction and by room type, but the key idea is that the code often distinguishes between spaces meant for regular occupancy and spaces that are more limited in use. That is why a tiny house may be able to get away with lower ceilings in some areas, especially under beams, in bathrooms, or in portions of lofts, while still needing a higher standard in the main floor area. If your design depends on shaving off every inch, you need to know where the code draws the line before the framing goes up.

Lofts are where a lot of tiny-house owners get into trouble, because a loft is not just a cute sleeping shelf. In the eyes of a building official, it may be treated as an occupied space with its own set of safety expectations. That means the loft may need enough ceiling height to be usable, enough floor area to count the way you want it to count, and enough access to get in and out without creating a hazard. Some codes are more flexible with lofts than with full rooms, but they still usually care about whether a person can stand, sit, or at least move safely in the space. A loft that looks perfect in a design rendering can become a problem if the code says the sleeping area is too low, too hard to reach, or too cramped to qualify the way you intended.

Access to the loft is another common flashpoint. A ladder might be fine in a casual conversation, but not every jurisdiction sees a ladder as an acceptable substitute for a stair. And even when a ladder is allowed, it may come with conditions about slope, width, handholds, tread design, or how securely it attaches. Stairs are usually easier to defend from a code perspective, but they take up more floor space, which is exactly what tiny-house builders are trying to save. That is why many designs use alternating tread stairs, ship ladders, or compact stair runs. The problem is that each of those options can trigger a different reaction from the local inspector. One office may view a narrow stair as a clever space-saving feature. Another may see it as a fall risk with no proper landing or handrail. If your project depends on an unconventional stair, it is smart to ask for the code basis in writing before you assume it will pass.

Egress is the safety issue that can override almost everything else. In plain English, egress means a way out in an emergency. For a sleeping area, that usually means a person must be able to escape quickly if there is a fire or other urgent hazard, and emergency responders must also have a realistic way to reach someone inside. In tiny houses, the egress question often comes up in lofts because they are common sleeping spaces. A loft may need a properly sized emergency exit window, or another approved escape route, depending on how the space is classified. A tiny home with a beautiful loft but no real emergency exit can run into serious problems at permit review, even if the rest of the structure looks solid. This is not just a technicality. If a sleeping area is too hard to escape from, the code will usually treat that as a real safety defect, not a design preference.

What makes these rules tricky is that they do not always work as a neat set. A loft might meet the height rule but fail the stair rule. A stair might be acceptable but eat enough space that the main floor ceiling no longer works with the overall layout. An egress window might be possible, but only if the wall height, framing, and roofline all cooperate. Tiny-house design is full of tradeoffs, and this is one of the places where the tradeoffs become legal, not just aesthetic. A builder can often solve one problem by changing another part of the plan, but that only works if the project is checked against the applicable code from the start instead of after the shell is built.

The safest way to think about these requirements is to treat them as a chain, not separate hurdles. Ceiling height affects whether a space is considered usable. Loft access affects whether that space is safely reachable. Egress affects whether someone can get out if something goes wrong. If one link is weak, the whole sleeping area may be questioned.

That is why tiny-house plans that look brilliant on paper sometimes need a redesign before they can survive review. The good news is that many code officials are more open to small-space solutions than people expect, as long as the plan shows that the design is intentional, measurable, and safe. The less you rely on guesswork, and the more you can point to the exact code issue you are solving, the better your odds of getting a yes instead of a long list of corrections.

Foundation-built tiny houses versus RV-style units

The legal difference between a tiny house on a foundation and an RV-style unit is not just about whether it has wheels. It is about what the law thinks the structure is for. A foundation-built tiny house is usually trying to enter the world as a real dwelling, which means it is judged under the same basic framework as other houses: zoning, building code, utilities, setbacks, and occupancy rules. An RV-style unit, by contrast, is usually treated as a movable vehicle or recreational unit, even if it looks a lot like a small home inside. That legal identity matters because a lot of local governments are willing to tolerate an RV in the right place for the right purpose, but not as a permanent residence on ordinary residential land.

This is where tiny-house buyers get tripped up. A structure can feel like a house, function like a house, and be beautifully finished like a house, but still be categorized as something else if it sits on a trailer chassis, is built to RV standards, or is marketed as "mobile." Once it falls into the RV bucket, the rules often shift away from residential building codes and toward vehicle or recreational standards. That can make the unit easier to manufacture and move, but harder to use as a long-term home. Many zoning codes do not allow RVs to be used as permanent dwellings outside of approved parks, campgrounds, temporary construction setups, or special exceptions. So the same space-saving design that makes an RV-style tiny house appealing can also make it legally fragile.

A foundation-built tiny house usually has the opposite problem. It is more likely to be accepted as a true residence, which is a big advantage if you want a permanent place to live. But that acceptance comes with the full weight of residential regulation. The structure may need to meet local building code requirements for foundations, anchoring, insulation, egress, stairs, smoke alarms, utility hookups, and minimum dwelling standards. If the house is built on a permanent foundation, officials are much more likely to ask whether it qualifies as a legal dwelling unit rather than a temporary shelter or portable unit. That can be good news, because it puts your tiny house in the same legal category as other homes. It can also be expensive, because once the law sees it as a house, it expects house-level compliance.

That distinction affects where you can place the unit. An RV-style tiny house may be allowed in an RV park, a licensed campground, or a temporary staging area, but not as the main residence on a standard suburban lot. A foundation-built tiny house may be allowed on a residential parcel, but only if the zoning allows a dwelling of that type and size. In some places, the foundation is what makes the project possible. In others, the foundation is what makes the project subject to stricter code review. Either way, the foundation is not just a construction choice. It is a legal signal. It tells the local government, “This is intended to stay here and function as a dwelling,” and that signal can open some doors while closing others.

Another practical difference shows up in permits and inspections. A foundation-built tiny house usually needs a building permit, approved plans, and multiple inspections during construction. Officials may want to see footing details, structural loads, utility connections, and proof that the home meets the local code for permanent occupancy. An RV-style unit may not go through the same building department process at all, because it may be certified under a different standard and sold through a different regulatory lane. But skipping the building code does not mean skipping the law. It often means moving into a different set of rules, and those rules may be more restrictive about where the unit can be parked, how long it can stay there, and whether anyone can legally sleep in it full time.

Insurance, financing, and resale also tend to follow this split. A foundation-built tiny house is more likely to be treated like real estate, which can help with traditional mortgages, property insurance, and long-term value. An RV-style unit is more likely to be treated like personal property, which may push you toward RV insurance, specialty lenders, or cash purchases. That does not make one option automatically better than the other, but it does change the legal and financial experience of owning it. If you want a house that can be sold like a house and insured like a house, the foundation route usually gives you a better shot. If you want mobility and a lower barrier to entry, the RV-style route may be more realistic, but you have to accept the limits that come with that classification.

There is also a gray area that causes constant confusion: some tiny houses are built to look like houses but are still legally RVs, while others are built on foundations but still face skepticism because of their size. Local officials may not care much about the aesthetic. They care about the legal category. A tiny house with shiplap walls and a farmhouse sink does not become a dwelling just because it looks charming. Likewise, a tiny house on a foundation does not automatically qualify for occupancy if the zoning code does not allow that use on the parcel. The key is to stop asking only, "Does it look like a house?" and start asking, "What legal category does this structure fall into, and what does that category allow here?"

That is the question that should shape your early decisions. If your goal is permanent living on a specific lot, a foundation-built tiny house is usually the cleaner legal path, even if it requires more paperwork and higher upfront cost. If your goal is mobility, flexibility, or temporary use, an RV-style unit may fit better, but you need to know that "easier to move" often means "harder to use as a permanent home." The structure itself is only half the story. The other half is whether your local rules are willing to recognize it as a place where someone can legally live.

When a tiny house must meet full residential code and when it may not

A tiny house does not automatically get to use the "small is simple" argument when it comes to code. In many places, the real question is not whether the house is tiny, but whether it is being treated as a dwelling that must perform like a full-time residence. If the answer is yes, then the project usually has to satisfy the same baseline expectations as any other home: safe structure, proper exits, adequate ceiling heights in required areas, sanitary facilities, and a level of durability that makes it fit for everyday living. The fact that the home is compact does not erase those requirements. It just makes them harder to meet in a small envelope.

That is why the legal path often turns on how the structure is classified from the start. A tiny house on a permanent foundation, connected to utilities, intended for year-round occupancy, and placed on a lot approved for residential use is much more likely to be treated as a full residential building. In that situation, the code official is not looking for a loophole. They are looking for compliance. The house may be small, but if it is acting like a house, the rules tend to follow suit. That usually means the project has to meet the local residential code or the state's adopted version of it, including any amendments that make the rules stricter.

By contrast, some tiny houses are allowed to avoid full residential code because they are not being treated as houses in the first place. That usually happens when the structure falls into a different legal category, such as an RV, a park model, a temporary structure, or a unit built under a separate manufactured-housing or specialty standard. Those categories can be useful, but they come with tradeoffs. A unit that is legally an RV may be allowed in an RV park or used for short-term or seasonal occupancy, but that does not mean it can be parked on a residential lot and used as a permanent home. A park model may be easier to place in a resort or campground setting, but that does not automatically make it a legal single-family dwelling. In other words, escaping full residential code usually means accepting a different identity with its own limits.

The biggest dividing line is often permanence. Once a tiny house is fixed to land, tied into utilities, and intended as the main residence, local officials are much more likely to expect full dwelling standards. Foundation, occupancy, and site approval all matter because they show the structure is not just a movable unit sitting temporarily on a parcel. Even if the house itself is built on a trailer frame, some jurisdictions will still look at how it is used and where it is placed. If the local code says a dwelling must be on a permanent foundation, then wheels can become a problem no matter how nicely the interior is finished. If the local code says only one dwelling unit is allowed per lot, then the issue may be zoning first and code second. The classification question and the occupancy question tend to feed each other.

There are also places where a tiny house may avoid full residential code because the local government has created a narrower path for small dwellings. Some jurisdictions adopt tiny-house-specific standards, often with reduced minimums for lofts, stairs, or square footage, especially for accessory dwelling units or small secondary homes. In those places, the house still has to be legal and safe, but it may not have to match every requirement of a conventional single-family home. That said, these exceptions are usually written carefully. They may apply only to a tiny house on a foundation, only within certain zoning districts, only as an accessory unit behind an existing home, or only if the structure is inspected and approved under a specific local ordinance. A tiny-house-friendly rule is still a rule, and it usually comes with strings attached.

A lot of confusion comes from the fact that "full residential code" is not always a single thing. In one town, it may mean the state residential code with local amendments. In another, it may mean a patchwork of adopted standards that borrows from model codes, fire regulations, plumbing rules, and energy rules. So when someone says a tiny house "has to meet code," the next question is always, which code, for what use, and in which jurisdiction? A tiny house may be exempt from one set of requirements and still have to satisfy another. For example, it might not need to meet every feature of a conventional house if it is classified as an accessory unit, but it may still need proper electrical, plumbing, and safety approvals before anyone can live in it.

The safest way to think about the issue is this: the more your tiny house looks like a permanent home, the more likely it is to be held to full residential standards. The more it looks like a movable or temporary unit, the more likely it is to be pushed into a separate category with narrower permission to occupy. Neither path is automatically easier. Full residential code can be demanding, but it often gives you the clearest legal footing for long-term living. Non-residential categories can be easier to build to in some respects, but they often come with restrictions on where you can place the unit, how long you can stay, and whether the structure can ever become a true home in the eyes of the law.

Chapter 5: Permits, Inspections, and Paperwork That Save You Headaches

Once you move from "Can I build this?" to "Can I actually get it approved and occupied?" the paper trail starts doing a lot of the heavy lifting. Permits, inspections, and the forms that go with them are not just bureaucratic clutter; they are the record that your tiny house was reviewed, accepted, and tracked through the system the local government uses to protect itself and you. That can feel slow, picky, and occasionally absurd, especially when you are dealing with a compact project that seems like it should be simpler than a full-size house.

The permit timeline from idea to occupancy

The permit timeline usually starts long before anyone hands you an application form. The earliest stage is the reality check: figuring out whether your idea fits the property, the zoning, and the code path you are trying to use. If you skip that step, you can waste weeks or months drawing plans for a project that cannot be approved as proposed. So before you pay for detailed construction drawings, it helps to identify the legal category you are aiming for: a foundation-built house, an accessory dwelling unit, a tiny house on wheels, a manufactured housing setup, or something else entirely. That choice shapes almost everything that follows, including which office reviews the plans, what documents they want, and whether you need one permit or several.

Once the path is clear enough, the next stage is pre-application contact. This is the part where you call, email, or visit the planning or building department and ask what they want to see before you submit. Some places are very organized and will give you a checklist. Others will answer in fragments, which is why it matters to get names, dates, and written responses whenever possible. A short conversation can save you from submitting the wrong set of plans or discovering too late that the parcel needs a zoning review, a utility signoff, or a separate septic approval. At this stage, you are not trying to argue your case. You are trying to learn the local sequence.

After that comes the actual permit application, and this is where tiny-house projects often slow down. A permit package may need site plans, floor plans, elevations, foundation details, structural information, energy compliance documents, and utility plans. If the project involves plumbing, electrical, septic, grading, or driveway access, those may trigger separate reviews or separate permits. The more your tiny house depends on custom design choices, the more likely the reviewer will ask for supporting documentation from a licensed professional. That does not mean your project is doomed. It means the office wants enough paper to prove the structure is safe, legal, and tied to a real site.

Review time is rarely a straight line. A permit can move from intake to technical review, then stall because one department is waiting on another. Planning may want to confirm land use before building can finish its review. Building may hold the permit until the septic permit is approved. Fire, public works, or utilities may each have their own comments. In a tiny-house project, the biggest source of delay is often not a flat no; it is a request for more information. That request can feel like a setback, but it is usually just the system asking you to fill a gap. The faster you respond with clear, complete answers, the faster the file usually moves again.

One thing many first-time builders underestimate is how much a permit timeline depends on the quality of the first submission. A clean, complete packet can move much faster than a technically correct but messy one. If the drawings are hard to read, if the site plan does not match the parcel records, or if the application leaves out a required detail, the reviewer may send it back instead of trying to guess what you meant. Tiny-house projects are especially vulnerable to this because they often sit in gray areas. If your plan is unusual, the department is going to look for reasons to slow down, not because they dislike tiny houses, but because unusual projects create more liability if something is missed.

Then comes the inspection phase, which is really a series of checkpoints rather than one final visit. Depending on the project, you may have inspections for footing or foundation work, framing, rough plumbing, rough electrical, insulation, drywall, final utility connections, and final occupancy. The order matters. If you cover something before it is inspected, you may have to open it back up. If the inspector cannot verify a required detail, the project may get a correction notice and another appointment. The best way to keep inspections from becoming a drama is to know what each inspector is looking for before they arrive, keep the site accessible, and make sure the approved plans are on hand.

The final step is not always called occupancy, but that is the practical goal: getting the official okay to live there. In some places that means a certificate of occupancy. In others it may be a final signoff, a use permit, or a utility release that effectively clears the home for habitation. This is the moment when the difference between "built" and "legal to occupy" becomes very real. A tiny house can be finished, furnished, and perfectly livable in a practical sense, but still not be approved for full-time occupancy if one required permit is missing or one final inspection has not passed. If you want the right to live there without looking over your shoulder, the occupancy signoff is the line that matters.

It also helps to expect that the timeline may expand if your project changes midstream. A bigger loft, a different foundation, a revised utility layout, or a switch from one legal category to another can trigger new review. That is why it is smart to treat the permit process as a living file, not a one-time formality. Every change should be checked against the permit before you build it. In tiny-house land, the shortest route to occupancy is usually not the fastest construction schedule. It is the clearest paper trail, the most complete application, and the least amount of surprise between the first idea and the final inspection.

Site plans, construction drawings, and supporting documents

Most permit offices do not want a creative sketch and a hopeful explanation. They want a paper trail that lets them answer the same basic questions every time: Where is the house going? What exactly is being built? How will it sit on the lot? How will people get in and out safely? That is why site plans, construction drawings, and supporting documents matter so much. They are not just part of the application packet; they are the proof that your tiny house project has been thought through in the language the local government understands.

The site plan is usually the first document that tells the story of the property. It shows the lot lines, the dimensions of the parcel, the location of the proposed tiny house, any existing structures, setbacks, driveways, utility connections, septic components, wells, easements, and sometimes drainage or grading details. For a tiny house, this sheet often becomes the make-or-break document because it answers a question that is bigger than the house itself: does this structure actually fit on this piece of land in a way that meets local rules? A lot of applications get delayed because the site plan is too vague, not to scale, or missing one of the things the reviewer needs to check, like the distance from the house to the property line or the location of the driveway access.

Construction drawings are the next layer down, and they need to be more than pretty floor plans. They usually include a floor plan, elevations, sections, foundation details, framing information, roof design, window and door schedules, and any special systems that make the house work. If the tiny house is on wheels, the drawings may need to show how the unit is secured, how it connects to utilities, and what parts are permanent versus movable. If it is on a foundation, the reviewer will usually want enough detail to understand the structural path from roof to footing. Tiny-house plans often fail here because the drawings look finished from a design standpoint but do not answer the code questions. A regulator is not trying to admire the layout. They are trying to see whether the structure can be built safely and legally.

One of the biggest mistakes people make is assuming that a builder's brochure or a decorative rendering can substitute for code-ready plans. It usually cannot. A permit reviewer may need dimensions, materials, structural notes, and installation details that never show up in a marketing packet. If your tiny house has a loft, a ladder, a compact stair, a special roof pitch, or an unusual window arrangement, those features need to be shown clearly enough that someone else could verify compliance without guessing. The more your project departs from a standard house shape, the more important it becomes to document how the design solves the usual code problems instead of just looking clever.

Supporting documents are where a lot of tiny-house applicants either save themselves or sink themselves. These are the extras that help the office connect the dots: survey maps, septic approvals, well permits, utility letters, engineered calculations, truss specs, energy forms, fire-safety notes, manufacturer documentation, and sometimes letters from a licensed professional. In some places, you may also need proof of ownership, HOA approval, a recorded easement, or a land-use approval before the building department will even look at the plans. If your tiny house is part of a larger legal strategy, the supporting documents often show that the project is not just a structure, but a lawful use of the land.

It helps to think of these documents as a chain. The site plan proves the house belongs on the lot. The construction drawings prove the house can be built as shown. The supporting documents prove the systems around it will also work. If one link is weak, the permit reviewer may stop there and ask for more. That does not always mean your project is doomed; it usually means the office cannot make the decision yet. A missing septic approval, for example, can stall an otherwise solid application because the house may be fine, but the place where it will live is not yet ready. Tiny-house projects often run into this kind of delay because the structure gets all the attention while the infrastructure gets left for later.

Good paperwork also protects you from the other common tiny-house problem: mismatched assumptions. A zoning officer may be thinking one thing, a building inspector another, and a utility provider something else entirely. Clear documents reduce the chance that each office imagines a different project. If the drawings say "accessory dwelling unit," the site plan shows the unit behind an existing home, and the utility plan shows separate service connections, everyone has a better shot at understanding the same proposal. If the paperwork is sloppy or contradictory, you may accidentally invite the exact confusion you were trying to avoid.

For tiny houses especially, it is smart to make sure every page tells the same legal story. The address, lot number, building type, foundation type, square footage, occupancy use, and utility setup should line up across the application, the drawings, and any outside approvals. A plan set that calls the project a "recreational unit" in one place and a "single-family dwelling" in another can create real trouble, because the office may decide you have not even identified the project correctly. Consistency is not glamorous, but in permit work it is often the difference between a quick review and a long round of questions.

Inspection checkpoints and how to prepare for them

Inspections are where a tiny-house project stops being theoretical. Up to that point, you can still live in the land of drawings, assumptions, and "we'll fix that later." An inspection is the moment an actual official looks at the work and decides whether it matches the approved plans and meets the code that applies. That means the best way to prepare is not to impress the inspector with charm or clever design. It is to make their job easy enough that they can say yes without having to guess what they are looking at.

The first thing to understand is that inspectors usually care about a very specific slice of the project, not the whole dream. One person may be checking the footing or foundation. Another may care only about framing, nailing patterns, or structural connections. Someone else may look at plumbing, electrical, HVAC, or final occupancy items. If your tiny house has a loft, a compact stair, or an unconventional layout, do not assume every inspector will read it the same way. Each visit is usually about one part of the build, and you should prepare for that part as if it is the only thing that matters that day.

The easiest way to avoid trouble is to keep the approved plans close and build to them exactly. If you made a change after the permit was issued, even a change that seems minor to you, ask whether it needs to be approved before the inspection. Tiny projects get into trouble when the field conditions drift away from the paperwork: a window moves, a wall thickness changes, a door swings differently, a loft railing is revised, or the utility layout gets adjusted on site. An inspector who sees something that does not match the permit set may stop the inspection, even if the change looks harmless. The rule of thumb is simple: if the paper says one thing and the house says another, expect a question.

Before each inspection, make the relevant parts of the work visible, accessible, and ready to examine. That sounds obvious, but a lot of failures happen because the thing being inspected is buried under something else. For framing, that means no insulation or drywall covering the area. For plumbing, it means clean access to the lines, shutoffs, traps, and fixtures. For electrical, it means open panels, labeled circuits if required, and no missing covers or unsafe temporary conditions. For foundation or anchoring work, it means the inspector can actually see the connections, fasteners, and any required documentation. If the inspector has to crawl over clutter or ask you to tear things apart just to view the work, you are already making the visit harder than it needs to be.

It also helps to have your paperwork organized before anyone arrives. Keep the permit card, approved plan set, revisions, manufacturer sheets, engineer letters, and any special approvals in one place. If your project depends on an alternate method, an exception, or a product listing, have that support ready too. Inspectors do not usually want a lecture, but they do appreciate being able to confirm that the thing they are looking at matches a code-approved detail or a permitted deviation. If a question comes up, being able to hand over the exact page or document saves time and can prevent a harmless misunderstanding from turning into a failed inspection.

Another smart move is to walk the project yourself before the official visit and look for the little things that often trigger corrections. Are smoke alarms installed where required and actually powered? Are handrails solid? Are stair treads consistent? Are guardrails complete? Are utility penetrations sealed? Are there exposed wires, loose fittings, missing labels, or unfinished edges that make the work look incomplete? A lot of inspection problems are not dramatic code violations. They are signs that the job is not quite finished, and inspectors are rarely eager to approve something that still looks like a work zone. If it looks temporary, they may treat it as temporary.

It is also worth learning the difference between a failed inspection and a request for clarification. Sometimes the inspector is not saying the project is doomed; they are saying they need more information or a correction before they can sign off. That is a useful distinction, because it changes how you respond. If the issue is factual, fix it and call for a reinspection. If the issue is interpretive, ask for the concern in writing and compare it to the permit conditions, code language, or approved plans. Stay calm and specific. "Can you show me exactly what needs to change?" is a much better question than "Why are you being so picky?"

Finally, remember that inspections are easier when the project has been built with the inspection sequence in mind. Tiny-house builders sometimes think in terms of finish work first because that is what makes the home feel real. Inspectors think in reverse. They want to verify the hidden stuff before it disappears, then confirm the visible stuff at the end. If you plan your build around those checkpoints, you save yourself from opening finished walls, undoing trim, or scrambling to prove that a detail was installed correctly. In tiny living, a smooth inspection is usually less about luck and more about respecting the order in which the law wants to see the house come together.

How to respond when a permit is denied or delayed

A permit denial or delay does not always mean your tiny house is dead in the water. A lot of the time, it means the reviewer saw a problem, or thought they saw a problem, and stopped the process until someone clears it up. That distinction matters. A denial can be a hard no, but it can also be a "not yet" dressed up in official language. Before you react emotionally, read the notice carefully and figure out whether the issue is about zoning, code, missing paperwork, or a mismatch between what you asked for and what the local rules actually allow. Those are very different problems, and they need very different responses.

The first move is to get the denial or delay in writing, if you do not already have it. If the office only told you verbally that your application is "incomplete" or "not approvable," ask for the exact reason and the specific rule behind it. You want names of code sections, ordinance references, missing documents, or technical objections. Vague feedback is hard to fix because it leaves you guessing. Specific feedback lets you decide whether the problem is simple, like a missing site plan note, or structural, like the property not allowing a second dwelling. If the official will not put it in writing, follow up by email so there is a record of what was said. Keep your tone calm and professional. You are building a paper trail, not a fight.

Once you know the reason, separate the fixable problems from the hard limits. A delay caused by missing signatures, unclear drawings, utility information, or an incomplete application packet is usually fixable. So is a plan set that needs a revision to show setbacks, roof pitch, stair details, or foundation information more clearly. A denial based on zoning, minimum dwelling size, or a prohibition on the type of unit you are proposing is a different animal. In that situation, the issue is not just paperwork. The project may need a different legal path, such as an accessory dwelling unit, a variance, a special-use permit, a different lot, or a different build style. If you keep resubmitting the same plan without addressing the real obstacle, you are just paying for another round of rejection.

If the problem is technical, fix it fast and cleanly. Do not send five pages of explanation when the office asked for one revised drawing. Do not argue with the reviewer over every note unless the note is actually wrong. Instead, answer the objection directly and make it easy for the staff member to see what changed. If the review comment says the plan does not show the location of the septic system, add that. If it says the loft access needs to meet a certain standard, revise the drawing and label it clearly. If your project depends on an interpretation, ask whether the office would accept a revised submittal that shows the project another way. Sometimes a small design adjustment solves a big bureaucratic problem without changing the spirit of the build.

If the problem is legal, not just technical, you have to decide whether to challenge the decision or work around it. That starts with reading the ordinance or code yourself, not relying only on someone's summary of it. Sometimes the denial is based on a rule that does not actually say what the reviewer thinks it says. Other times the reviewer is right, and the code simply does not support your plan. If you believe the office got it wrong, ask for the appeal process, the deadline, and the exact body that hears the appeal. Many jurisdictions have a board of adjustment, planning commission, building official review, or another path for reconsideration. Appeals are usually time-sensitive, so do not sit on the letter while you debate whether you "should" push back.

When you do challenge a denial, keep your argument narrow and grounded in the text. Point to the specific ordinance language, code section, or approved precedent that supports your position. Bring documents, not drama. A short, organized packet usually works better than a long emotional letter. If you have emails from staff, prior approvals, or examples of similar projects that were approved under the same rule, include them. Just be careful not to assume that one neighbor's success guarantees yours. Officials care a lot about the exact facts of the parcel, the district, and the application. Your job is to show why your project fits the rule as written, or why the denial misread the rule.

Delays need their own strategy because they can quietly drain a project even when nobody says no. If your file is stuck, ask where it is in the process and what is still outstanding. Sometimes the hold-up is internal and has nothing to do with your application. A reviewer may be waiting for another department, a supervisor may need sign-off, or the office may be short-staffed. In those cases, polite persistence helps. Send a concise follow-up, restate the application number, and ask whether anything else is needed from you to move it forward. If weeks pass without movement, ask whether there is a formal status update process. Keep a log of dates, names, and responses so you can see whether the delay is normal or becoming unreasonable.

There is also a practical point that tiny-house builders learn the hard way: sometimes the best response to a denial is not to keep forcing the same application. It is to change the strategy. That might mean shifting from a full-time dwelling to an ADU, moving from a wheeled unit to a foundation-built structure, choosing a different lot, or getting a planner, designer, or code consultant involved before you resubmit. The goal is not to "win" against the office. The goal is to get to a project that can actually be approved and lived in legally. If you treat the denial as useful information instead of a personal insult, you can often turn a dead end into a better route.

Chapter 6: Choosing the Right Legal Path for Your Tiny House

Once you know the rules on the ground, the next question is less about whether a tiny house can exist legally and more about which legal lane it should live in. That choice matters because the category you pick shapes almost everything that follows: what kind of approvals you chase, how much flexibility you have with the site, and how the project will be treated by people who have never seen your floor plan but still need to stamp a form. A tiny house can look similar from the outside and still be handled very differently depending on whether it is being positioned as a movable unit, a permanent dwelling, a secondary home, or something else entirely.

Tiny house on wheels, foundation home, ADU, or manufactured housing

The first thing to sort out is what kind of legal creature your tiny house is supposed to be, because the answer changes everything else. A tiny house on wheels, a foundation home, an ADU, and a manufactured home are not just different styles of the same idea. They live in different parts of the legal system, and each one comes with its own set of rules, approvals, and headaches. If you pick the wrong category for your project, you can end up designing a beautiful home that does not fit the paperwork, or paperwork that does not fit the home.

A tiny house on wheels is usually the most mobile-looking option, but legally it often gets treated as something other than a house. Depending on the jurisdiction, it may be viewed as a trailer, RV, park model, or movable dwelling. That matters because a unit with wheels can trigger transportation rules, vehicle registration issues, RV park restrictions, and limits on long-term occupancy. In some places, the fact that it can move is exactly why it is not allowed as a permanent residence on a residential lot. In others, the wheels are less important than whether the unit is connected to utilities, anchored, and used as a dwelling. The legal problem is that "tiny house on wheels" is a design description, not a legal category with one universal meaning.

A foundation home is usually the cleanest path if your goal is to live in the structure as a true house. Once the building is permanently attached to land, local officials are much more likely to process it under ordinary residential rules. That can mean standard zoning for a single-family home, or it can mean the project needs to fit within a lot's minimum size, setback, height, and occupancy requirements. The upside is that a foundation home is easier to explain to a permit office, lender, insurer, or future buyer. The downside is that you lose the flexibility of mobility, and you usually have to meet the full expectations that come with a permanent dwelling: site work, foundation design, utility connections, and code compliance that looks a lot more like a conventional house than a clever compact build.

An ADU, or accessory dwelling unit, sits in a different lane altogether. Instead of asking, "Can this tiny house be a house at all?" the law is asking, "Can this be a second dwelling on a lot that already has a primary residence?" That distinction is huge. Many places that would never allow a tiny house as a standalone home are much more open to an ADU because the use is already familiar to the zoning code. The catch is that ADUs are usually tied to a lot with an existing main house, and they often have their own limits on size, height, parking, owner occupancy, entrance placement, and utility connections. In other words, an ADU can be a friendlier legal pathway, but it is not a blank check. It is a regulated exception to the normal one-house-per-lot setup.

Manufactured housing is another category that gets confused with tiny houses all the time, but it has its own formal system. A manufactured home is built to federal standards under the HUD code, not the same code path used for a site-built house. That can be helpful because the standards are clear and widely recognized, and the home is designed to be transported from a factory to a site. But it also means the unit must actually fit the manufactured-home definition to be treated that way. A lot of tiny houses do not. If a structure is too small, too custom, or built outside the HUD manufactured-home framework, calling it "manufactured housing" will not magically make it one. Regulators care about certification labels, construction standards, and whether the unit was built under the right program, not just whether it came from a factory.

From a legal strategy standpoint, the best category is usually the one your property and local rules already know how to handle. If the lot supports an ADU, that may be the smoothest route. If the project is meant to be a permanent residence on its own parcel, a foundation home may be the most defensible. If mobility is the point, a tiny house on wheels may fit your lifestyle better, but it may also narrow your legal options for where you can stay. And if you are considering manufactured housing, you need to know whether the home is actually built and certified under that system, because the label has real consequences. The mistake people make is choosing the category based on aesthetics or ideology instead of legal fit.

This is also where financing and insurance start to follow the category, not just the square footage. Lenders are usually more comfortable with a foundation home or an ADU because those fit familiar property and collateral models. A tiny house on wheels may be harder to finance as real estate because it may not be real estate in the first place. Insurance companies ask similar questions: Is it a dwelling, a vehicle, an RV, a manufactured home, or a site-built structure? If you cannot answer clearly, they may not be able to either. That is why it helps to decide early whether your project is trying to be movable, permanent, accessory, or factory-built. The answer shapes not only legality, but also the practical ability to live in the thing without constant second-guessing.

Before you get too far into design decisions, it helps to force the project into one of these buckets on paper and then test whether the bucket matches the parcel, the zoning, and the permit path. If it does not, changing the roofline or shaving off a few square feet will not fix the real problem. The legal category is the foundation under the whole plan, even when the home itself sits on wheels.

Pros and cons of each legal pathway

Every legal path for a tiny house is a trade-off. The question is not which option is "best" in the abstract. It is which option gives you the cleanest mix of legality, cost, flexibility, and long-term sanity for the way you actually want to live. A tiny house on wheels, a foundation-built tiny home, an accessory dwelling unit, and manufactured housing all solve different problems. They also create different problems. If you choose a path because it sounds simpler, cheaper, or more independent, you can end up paying for that choice later in permits, financing, insurance, resale, or plain old daily convenience.

A tiny house on wheels is often the most flexible option on paper and the least predictable in practice. The big advantage is mobility. If your land situation changes, if you want to move closer to work, or if you are testing a lifestyle before committing to a permanent site, wheels can feel like freedom. In some places, that mobility also gives you a way to avoid full residential code, because the unit may be treated more like an RV or park model than a house. But that same legal identity is the downside. Many zoning codes do not want an RV used as a full-time residence outside of very specific settings. Some counties will allow it only in campgrounds, RV parks, or temporary situations. Financing can be tough, insurance can be limited, and resale depends heavily on whether the next buyer has a place to put it legally. The house may be small, but the legal uncertainty can be huge.

A foundation-built tiny house usually has the strongest claim to being a real home, which is a big advantage if your goal is long-term occupancy on a specific piece of land. Once a tiny house is attached to a foundation and designed as a permanent dwelling, it can fit more naturally into the ordinary housing system. That can make zoning, utilities, and resale feel more straightforward, especially in places that already allow small homes or accessory dwellings. It may also open the door to standard mortgage options more easily than a movable unit. The trade-off is that you lose a lot of the freedom people associate with tiny living. A foundation home is usually more expensive to site, permit, and build to code. You may need full compliance with residential requirements, which can mean stairs, ceiling heights, insulation, energy rules, and utility hookups that eat into the “tiny” simplicity. If the local zoning does not like small detached homes, being on a foundation does not magically fix that.

Accessory dwelling units, or ADUs, are often the most legally comfortable route when they are available. That is because the law already understands the concept: a smaller secondary home on a lot that already has a primary residence. If your property is in a city or county that welcomes ADUs, you may find the path smoother than trying to introduce a brand-new housing type. The biggest upside is that ADUs often have clearer rules than other tiny-house categories. The zoning code may already spell out setbacks, size limits, parking rules, and occupancy requirements. That makes planning less of a guessing game. The downside is that ADUs are not a free-for-all. They usually require a main house on the lot, and they often have specific size caps, design limits, and utility requirements. They also tend to be location-dependent, meaning a city that loves ADUs may be friendly while the next town over still treats them like a nuisance. If you do not already own a suitable lot with a primary dwelling, this path may not be available at all.

Manufactured housing sits in a different category altogether, and that can be both a strength and a limitation. The strength is that manufactured homes have an established legal and industry framework. That means clearer standards, more familiar financing options in many cases, and a more predictable path than a highly customized tiny-house build. If your main goal is to live small without constantly explaining your home to every official, lender, and insurer, that clarity can be valuable. The downside is that manufactured housing is not the same thing as a custom tiny house, and it may not give you the design freedom you want. Size, appearance, transport, and installation rules can all affect whether it works for your vision. Some people also resist the label because they want the aesthetics or craftsmanship of a bespoke tiny house, not a factory-built unit. And even when the housing category is clear, zoning can still limit where it can go.

The biggest hidden difference between these paths is not the building itself. It is the legal ecosystem around it. A wheel-based unit may let you move faster, but it often lives in a more fragile legal category. A foundation home may be easier to defend as a dwelling, but it usually demands more code compliance and more site investment. An ADU may be the smoothest approval route, but only if your property and local code already support it. Manufactured housing may offer a more established lane, but it comes with its own standards and may not match your ideal build style. So the real choice is not just about what you want to live in. It is about what kind of legal burden you are willing to carry every time you build, insure, finance, move, or sell.

It also helps to think about your exit plan before you choose a category. If you expect to stay put for decades, a foundation-built tiny house or ADU may be worth the extra approval work because the legal stability can pay off over time. If you are still figuring out where you want to land, a tiny house on wheels may protect your flexibility, even if it makes some other parts of life harder. If your priority is getting into a small home with the fewest surprises, manufactured housing may be the least romantic but most organized route. None of these paths is automatically right or wrong. The better question is which one matches your tolerance for red tape, your budget for compliance, and your willingness to live with the category the law gives your home, not just the one you give it yourself.

How financing, insurance, and resale value change by category

The legal category you choose does not just affect whether you can park or build a tiny house. It also changes how lenders, insurers, and future buyers see the project. That matters because a tiny house is not only a place to live; it is also an asset, and different legal categories make that asset look safer, riskier, or harder to value. A house that is treated like real estate usually gets a very different financial life than one treated like a trailer, a recreational unit, or a custom structure with no standard market category.

If your tiny house is built on a permanent foundation and recognized as a dwelling, financing is usually the easiest of the three areas. Traditional mortgage lenders are still picky, but they understand real property better than they understand movable housing. They know how to appraise land and improvements, they know how to secure a loan with a mortgage, and they have established procedures for underwriting. That does not mean a tiny foundation home is automatically easy to finance. Size can still create appraisal problems, and some lenders get nervous if the home is far smaller than the neighborhood norm. But the structure at least lives in a familiar legal lane, which gives you a better shot at conventional financing, construction loans, or refinance options later on.

Tiny houses on wheels usually sit in a tougher financing category because they are often treated more like personal property than real estate. That means you may be looking at a chattel loan, a personal loan, a credit union product, or cash. Those loans can work, but they often come with shorter terms, higher interest rates, and less favorable repayment structures than a mortgage. Lenders also worry about what happens if the unit is moved, damaged, or difficult to repossess. From their perspective, a movable tiny house can be harder to secure than a house attached to land. If you are planning to buy land separately, that can create a second financing problem too, because the land loan and the house financing may not line up neatly.

Insurance follows a similar pattern. A tiny house that is legally a home on a foundation is usually easier to place into standard homeowners insurance, though the insurer may still ask questions about square footage, construction quality, utilities, and occupancy. If the house is a legal dwelling, the insurer can usually fit it into a familiar risk model, even if it is unusually small. But if the unit is on wheels, the policy picture often shifts toward RV insurance, personal property coverage, or a specialized tiny-house policy. Those policies can be useful, but they are not always a perfect match for how people actually use the unit. Some cover travel and road risks better than long-term occupancy. Others may exclude certain damage, limit full-time living, or require the unit to meet specific standards before they will write the policy.

The biggest insurance problem is not always whether you can get a policy. It is whether the policy matches the way the tiny house is legally and practically used. If a unit is marketed or insured as an RV but is being used as a year-round residence on a lot that the local government does not recognize for that purpose, you can end up with a bad mismatch. The insurer may not care about zoning on day one, but it may care a great deal when there is a claim. If the house was misrepresented, used outside the policy terms, or built in a category the insurer did not intend to cover, a denial or reduced payout becomes a real risk. The same goes for foundation homes that are occupied before final approvals or before the structure is properly classified. The cleaner your legal category, the cleaner your insurance conversation usually is.

Resale value is where the category question becomes very visible. A tiny house that is legally a dwelling on land can often be sold more like a small home, which opens the door to a broader pool of buyers and more predictable valuation. Buyers can compare it to other real property, look at location, utilities, and site improvements, and potentially use mortgage financing. That tends to support resale value, even if the home is unconventional. By contrast, a tiny house on wheels often has a smaller resale market because the buyer is not just purchasing a house; they are purchasing a movable unit with a narrower set of financing and placement options. That limits the number of people who can realistically buy it, which can soften the price on resale.

There is also a difference between what the house is worth to you and what it is worth to a buyer. Tiny-house owners often put a lot of money into custom finishes, clever storage, and design details that feel priceless in daily life. The market may not reward those features dollar for dollar. If the unit is legally hard to place, hard to insure, or hard to finance, buyers will discount it no matter how beautiful it is. On the other hand, if the tiny house has a clear legal path, proper permits, documented construction, and a category that lenders and insurers understand, those paper details can do as much for resale value as fancy cabinetry. In tiny-house real estate, paperwork is part of the product.

That is why the category decision should be made with the long game in mind. A wheel-based unit may give you flexibility and lower upfront barriers, but it can also limit your financing choices, complicate insurance, and narrow your resale market. A foundation-built tiny home may take more effort to approve, but it often gives you a more stable financial profile. If you are trying to decide between categories, it helps to ask a blunt question: do you want the most freedom now, or the most mainstream financial treatment later? In tiny-house law, those two goals do not always point in the same direction.

Questions to ask before committing to a build style

Before you lock yourself into a build style, get brutally honest about what problem you are trying to solve. Are you trying to live full-time on one parcel? Move the house later? Avoid full residential code? Keep financing options open? Use a backyard lot? The right build style is not just the one that looks the best or costs the least up front. It is the one that matches the legal path you actually have access to. A lot of tiny-house regret comes from choosing a structure first and a legal category second. By then, you may already be stuck trying to force a square peg into a zoning code that never wanted it.

One of the first questions to ask is whether mobility is truly a feature you need or just a nice idea. A tiny house on wheels sounds flexible, but that flexibility can come with legal baggage. In many places, wheels push the unit toward RV, trailer, or transportable-structure treatment, which can limit where it can be parked and how long it can stay there. If you do not actually plan to move it, you may be paying for a mobility advantage you will never use while giving up the easier legal treatment that sometimes comes with a permanent foundation. On the other hand, if you need the option to relocate the home, a foundation can become a trap. Ask yourself whether the build style supports your real life, not your fantasy version of it.

Next, ask what the local government is most likely to recognize as a dwelling. That sounds obvious, but it is where a lot of projects go sideways. Some places are far more comfortable with a tiny house if it is built on a permanent foundation and tied into the property like a conventional house or ADU. Other places have clearer pathways for accessory units than for movable dwellings. Still others may allow a tiny house on wheels only in a specific park, rural setting, or temporary use arrangement. The key question is not "Can I build this?" but "What category does this local code already know how to approve?" The more your build style lines up with a familiar category, the less you have to convince officials to invent a new one for you.

You also want to ask how the build style affects code compliance. A foundation-built tiny house may need to satisfy more of the standard residential code, which can mean more certainty but also more requirements. A wheeled unit may avoid some building-code issues but run into vehicle or occupancy limits instead. If your design depends on very low ceilings, steep ladders, or a compact bathroom layout, you need to know whether those choices are acceptable under the code path you are choosing. Do not assume "tiny" automatically means "exempt." Ask which rules still apply, which ones can be modified, and which ones are nonnegotiable. That answer should shape the design before the first serious drawing is done.

Financing is another big question, because the build style can change whether the project looks like real estate, personal property, or something in between. Lenders tend to like predictability. So do insurers. A tiny house that is legally treated like a house on land may be easier to finance and insure than one classified as a movable unit. But that is not always the right trade-off if your goal is flexibility or lower entry cost. Ask what category the build style will likely fall into after completion, and whether that category helps or hurts your long-term plan. If you think you might sell later, you should also ask how a future buyer will see the property. A legal structure that is easy to explain is usually easier to sell.

Site conditions matter too, and they can quietly eliminate certain build styles before you even get to the design stage. Does the lot have space for setbacks, parking, utility hookups, septic, or a foundation? Is the road suitable for delivery? Is the parcel in a floodplain, hillside area, or place with soil issues that make one type of construction more practical than another? A tiny house on wheels may seem simpler until you discover the site has nowhere legal to park it. A foundation may seem more permanent until the soil report or utility requirements make it expensive or slow. Ask whether the land supports the structure you want, not just whether the structure supports your taste.

It also helps to ask how much future flexibility you want to preserve. Some build styles give you cleaner legal footing but fewer escape routes. Others give you more movement but more uncertainty. If your plan is to start small, live in the unit temporarily, and later convert or expand, you need to know whether the local rules allow that kind of transition. Can a wheeled tiny house later become a permitted dwelling? Can a temporary unit be upgraded to a permanent one? Can an ADU be detached now and expanded later? These are not just design questions. They are legal questions about whether your project can evolve without starting over.

Before you commit, ask the simplest question of all: what would make this choice a mistake in two years? If the answer is "I can't get a permit," that points you toward a build style that fits existing code better. If the answer is "I can't move it," that points you away from a permanent foundation. If the answer is "I can't finance or insure it," that may rule out a category that looks good on paper but creates too much friction later. The best build style is usually the one that survives the most boring questions. Boring is good here. Boring means the project has a chance of being legal, livable, and still standing when the novelty wears off.

Chapter 7: Finding a Place to Live Legally

Before you commit to a parcel, a rental, or a "temporary" landing spot, you need to know whether the place can actually support the kind of tiny living you have in mind. This is where the dream meets the dirt. A property can look perfect on paper and still be a dead end once you start asking who controls it, what kind of dwelling is allowed there, and whether the site can realistically support day-to-day living without constant rule-breaking. The goal here is not to turn every search into a legal seminar; it is to help you stop wasting time on locations that were never going to work and focus your energy on places that have a real chance of passing the smell test.

How to vet a property before you buy or rent

Before you buy or rent anything, treat the property like a legal puzzle, not a real estate listing. The photos, the price, and the seller's pitch are almost never the important part. What matters is whether that parcel can legally support the kind of tiny living you want, and whether the site has the basic infrastructure and approvals to make daily life realistic. A lot of tiny-house disappointment starts with a property that looks perfect on the surface but has one hidden problem that shuts the whole plan down: no legal dwelling allowed, no sewer capacity, no road access, no water source, or private restrictions that make your intended use impossible.

The first thing to verify is the property's permitted use. Do not settle for a vague answer like "it's residential" or "people live there now." You want the actual zoning designation and the specific rules tied to that parcel. Ask whether the lot allows one dwelling, more than one dwelling, accessory dwelling units, manufactured housing, RV-style occupancy, or only a seasonal structure. If your tiny house is on wheels, ask whether it can be parked there as a residence or only stored there. If it is on a foundation, ask whether the code path treats it as a house, a secondary unit, or something that still needs a special approval. The key question is not "Can a tiny house exist here?" It is "Can this exact kind of tiny house be used here the way I want to use it?"

Next, check the property's private restrictions. A parcel can be perfectly fine under public zoning and still be blocked by a deed restriction, covenant, HOA rule, or land-use agreement. These private rules are easy to ignore until they become your problem. Ask for the deed, the title report, any recorded covenants, and the current HOA documents if there is an association. Look for language about minimum square footage, single-family use, parking restrictions, RV bans, guest-house limits, or approval rights for exterior changes and additional dwellings. If you are renting, ask for the lease addendum or park rules in writing. A landlord or park manager saying "we're flexible" is not the same as having written permission to live there legally.

Then move to the site itself. Even if the land is zoned correctly, the parcel still has to function as a place to live. That means checking water, sewer or septic, electricity, trash service, and road access. If the property relies on a septic system, find out whether it is permitted for the number of bedrooms or occupants you want, and whether it can handle an additional dwelling. If there is a well, ask whether it is shared, permitted, and adequate. If you plan to use solar, composting toilets, or holding tanks, do not assume that makes the site automatically legal. Some jurisdictions care less about your preferred setup and more about whether the property has approved sanitation and utility arrangements. Also check whether emergency vehicles can reach the site, because access issues can come up as both a safety and permitting problem.

Pay close attention to lot size, setbacks, and placement limits. A property can be "buildable" in a general sense and still be too tight for the structure you want once you account for required distances from property lines, other buildings, wells, septic fields, or easements. That matters especially if you are hoping to add a tiny house as a second unit or place one in a backyard. A lot that looks roomy may still be legally crowded once the survey is measured against the code. If possible, get a survey or at least a site plan before you commit. Do not rely on memory, aerial photos, or a seller's rough estimate of where the boundaries are. Tiny-house projects live and die by inches more often than people expect.

It also helps to ask about the property's history. Has anyone ever applied for a permit there? Was a tiny house, ADU, mobile home, or accessory structure previously approved or denied? Has the county cited the parcel for occupancy issues, septic failures, or unpermitted structures? Past enforcement does not always mean the site is unusable, but it can tell you how the local office is likely to react when you show up with your plans. A property with a history of failed permit attempts may come with a built-in headache, while a parcel that has already supported a legal secondary unit may give you a much smoother path.

If you are renting, the vetting process needs one extra layer of caution: make sure the person offering the space actually has the authority to let you use it the way you intend. A landowner may be able to rent a pad, a backyard spot, or a rural lot, but that does not automatically mean the arrangement is lawful for full-time occupancy. Ask whether the jurisdiction recognizes the setup as long-term housing, whether the utilities are approved for that use, and whether the arrangement could be shut down by zoning, code enforcement, or the park's own rules. If the answer comes back fuzzy, get nervous. Tiny-house renters get burned when they assume "temporary" means "safe," only to find out the property was never approved for sleeping, sanitation, or permanent residence at all.

A good habit is to ask every important question in a way that forces a yes, no, or written explanation. For example: "Is a tiny house on wheels allowed as a dwelling on this parcel?" "Is an accessory dwelling unit permitted by right?" "Does the septic system support a second residence?" "Are there deed restrictions that limit additional housing?" "Can you send me the relevant ordinance section or approval in writing?" If the answer is vague, that is information too. A property is only a good candidate if the legal path is clear enough that you are not relying on hope, rumor, or someone's casual interpretation of the rules.

Tiny house-friendly communities, parks, and land-sharing options

One of the easiest ways to make tiny living work legally is to stop thinking only in terms of "my land" and start thinking in terms of "someone else's system." Tiny house-friendly communities, parks, and land-sharing setups are all built around that idea. Instead of trying to force a tiny house onto a random parcel and hoping the rules cooperate, you are looking for places where the rules, the infrastructure, and the expectations already lean in your favor. That can save a huge amount of time, money, and emotional damage.

Tiny house communities come in a few flavors. Some are private developments built specifically for small homes, with lot leases, shared roads, and community rules that spell out what is allowed. Others are informal clusters on private land, where a landowner has carved out spaces for multiple tiny homes, often with shared utilities or common amenities. Some are more like RV parks that have opened the door to tiny houses on wheels, either seasonally or full-time. And some are mixed housing arrangements where tiny homes sit alongside cabins, cottages, or other small dwellings under a local approval structure that already recognizes more than one unit on a property.

The appeal is obvious. If a community is already designed for tiny living, you are less likely to run into the usual "this is not allowed here" problem. The roads may be built for smaller units, the septic system may be sized for multiple dwellings, and the operator may already know how to handle questions about hookups, occupancy, and address assignment. In a good setup, you are not educating the entire local government from scratch every time you ask a question. That does not mean there are no rules. It usually means the rules are clearer, and the path to compliance is easier to see.

Still, "tiny-house-friendly" does not automatically mean "anything goes." A community can be welcoming and still have strict requirements about what kind of unit you bring in, how it is built, and whether it must be on wheels, on a permanent foundation, or certified in a particular way. Some places accept only RVIA-certified units or park models. Others allow foundation-built tiny homes but not mobile ones. Some communities market themselves to tiny-house buyers but quietly rely on local zoning allowances that only work because the operator has already secured approvals for a specific use. If you are considering one of these places, the key question is not just whether tiny houses are welcome, but what legal category the community is actually operating under.

That same caution applies to tiny house parks. A park can be a great option when you want a legal place to live without buying a full-sized lot, but the details matter. Are you renting a space month to month, or signing a long-term lease? Is the park approved for permanent residence, or only for temporary stays? Are utilities included, separately metered, or capped? Are there restrictions on skirting, decks, porches, sheds, pets, or guest stays? A park that looks simple on a website can turn out to have a very specific set of operating rules once you read the lease or park handbook. And if the park is in a jurisdiction that treats tiny homes as recreational units, you need to know whether the park's approval depends on that classification staying intact.

Land-sharing is a little different, and often more flexible. In a land-sharing arrangement, one property owner allows another person to place a tiny house on the land, sometimes with a rental agreement, sometimes through a partnership, and sometimes under a more informal setup that should really be formalized before anyone moves in. This can work well in rural areas, on larger residential lots, or on agricultural land where the owner wants to make better use of the property. It can also be a smart path for people who want community without buying a whole parcel. But because the arrangement is private, the legal structure matters a lot. You want to know who owns the land, who owns the tiny house, who pays for utilities, what happens if the relationship ends, and whether the local rules even allow the arrangement in the first place.

If you are exploring any of these options, the paperwork deserves as much attention as the scenery. Ask for the community rules, lease, or membership agreement before you commit. Look for language about occupancy limits, utility responsibility, vehicle registration, fire access, setbacks, and whether the unit must stay mobile. If you are dealing with a land-sharing deal, get clear on whether you are a tenant, a guest, a co-owner, or something else entirely. That distinction can affect eviction rights, insurance, tax treatment, and what happens if the property changes hands. A friendly handshake deal may feel low-stress at first, but tiny-house living has a way of becoming complicated right when everyone wishes it had been put in writing.

It also helps to ask how the site interacts with local government. A community may be private, but it still has to fit within the surrounding zoning, health, and safety rules. Ask whether the operator has already worked with the county or city on approvals, whether the water and septic systems are permitted, and whether the address can support mail delivery, emergency response, and utility accounts. If the answer to those questions is vague, that is a warning sign. The best tiny-house-friendly places are not just attractive; they are built on a legal foundation sturdy enough to keep the whole setup from wobbling the first time a code inspector, utility company, or neighbor asks a hard question.

Utility hookups, septic systems, water access, and road access

Utilities are one of those boring details that can make or break a tiny house plan. People often focus on the structure itself, but the site is usually where the real legal drama starts. A tiny house may be perfectly built and still be a dead end if the lot cannot legally connect to power, water, sewer, or a road that emergency vehicles can use. Local officials care about these systems because they are not just conveniences. They are tied to health, safety, access, and whether the property can support a lawful dwelling in the first place.

Electric hookup is usually the easiest piece to understand, but even that can be more complicated than it sounds. If the tiny house is going on a foundation and treated like a residence, the utility company may want a standard service connection, proper meter placement, and a clear path for inspection and approval. If the house is on wheels or designed more like a movable unit, the utility provider may still be willing to supply power, but the local code may not treat that connection as proof that the unit is legal to occupy. In other words, getting electricity to the site does not automatically solve zoning or occupancy issues. It only solves the part about having electricity.

Water access can be just as important, and sometimes more sensitive. Some parcels have municipal water available at the street, which sounds simple until you find out the connection fee is steep, the line must be extended, or the local rules require a certain minimum dwelling type before a tap can be approved. Other properties rely on a private well, which brings its own set of questions: Is the well permitted? Is it adequate for the intended number of occupants? Does the health department need to sign off? In rural areas, a well can be the difference between a workable tiny-house site and a property that looks usable but cannot support full-time living without major upgrades.

Septic systems are where tiny-house dreams often meet the hard reality of sanitation law. If a parcel is not served by municipal sewer, the local health department or environmental agency usually wants to know exactly how wastewater will be handled. A septic permit is rarely about the tiny house alone; it is about the whole site, the soil, the setback distances, the number of bedrooms or sleeping spaces, and the system's capacity. That means a tiny house with a clever layout can still trigger a surprisingly serious septic review if the county counts the loft as a sleeping area or sees the project as a full-time residence. Composting toilets and other alternative systems may be allowed in some places, but they are not a universal workaround. A lot depends on whether the local authority recognizes them as part of a legal sanitation plan or just as a side feature.

One of the biggest mistakes tiny-house buyers make is assuming that "off-grid" means "outside the rules." It usually does not. A lack of utility hookups can raise even more questions, not fewer. Officials may want to know how you will handle potable water, wastewater, trash storage, fire safety, and winter conditions. If you are using solar power, rainwater collection, a holding tank, or a composting toilet, the question is not whether those systems sound sustainable. The question is whether the local code, health department, and zoning rules allow them for the specific use you want. Some places are open to alternative systems. Others accept them only in limited circumstances, such as seasonal use, agricultural land, or properties with special permits.

Road access is another issue that sounds simple until you run into the details. A lot of tiny-house projects fail not because the house is too small, but because the lot is too hard to reach. Local governments want to know whether the property has legal access from a public road, whether the driveway meets width and slope requirements, and whether emergency vehicles can get in and out safely. A long private lane, a narrow easement, a seasonal road, or a shared access strip can all create problems. If a fire truck, ambulance, or utility crew cannot reasonably reach the site, that can become a serious obstacle to permits, occupancy, or even financing.

For tiny houses on wheels, road access can raise a different kind of issue. If the unit is going to be delivered by trailer, the route itself may matter. Low bridges, tight turns, weight limits, and local towing restrictions can all affect whether the house can actually get to the property without special arrangements. After delivery, the same road conditions may affect whether the unit can legally remain there if it is treated as a movable structure. A parcel that seems fine in a map search may turn out to be a nightmare for access once you look at the physical road, the legal easements, and the local emergency requirements.

The safest way to think about utilities and access is to treat them as proof points, not assumptions. Ask who provides power, water, and sewer service in that area. Ask whether the parcel is already connected or whether new service will require permits, inspections, or upgrades. Ask the health department what kind of septic approval is needed. Ask the fire department or planning office whether the road and driveway meet access standards. A property that can answer those questions cleanly is far more likely to support a legal tiny house than one that relies on vague promises, informal arrangements, or "we've always done it this way" explanations from a seller.

Red flags that suggest a location will never work legally

Some places are not "hard" to legalize. They are basically impossible. The trick is spotting that before you spend money on surveys, drawings, deposits, or a tiny house delivery fee. A lot of tiny-house buyers talk themselves into a bad site because they assume the right paperwork, the right attitude, or the right workaround will eventually make it fit. Sometimes that is true. But if the property is fighting you on every front, the smarter move is to walk away early.

The biggest red flag is a zoning code that clearly allows only one dwelling unit and does not offer a clean path for a second one. If the lot already has a house on it and the zoning does not allow an accessory dwelling unit, a second principal dwelling, or some other approved exception, that is not a small obstacle. It is usually the core problem. When the code says one home per lot and the officials have no reason to bend, your tiny house is not "almost approved." It is a second residence that the land use rules do not want.

Another warning sign is a property with private restrictions that are stricter than the city. If there is a homeowners association, a deed restriction, a covenant, or a neighborhood agreement that limits minimum house size, bans secondary dwellings, or requires all homes to match a certain style, you can end up with a perfectly legal municipal approval that still does not let you live there. Private restrictions are especially frustrating because they are often buried in closing documents or recorded paperwork that people never read closely. If the seller says, "The county is fine with it," that is not enough. You need to know whether the property itself has private rules that shut the door.

Road access problems are another giant warning. If the site cannot legally support emergency access, utility service, or a permitted driveway, the rest of the plan can collapse fast. A parcel that looks peaceful and secluded may be a nightmare if it is landlocked, served by a narrow easement, or connected by a road that the county will not recognize for residential use. Tiny-house projects often depend on the assumption that "we can figure out access later," but access is not a side issue. If fire trucks, ambulances, inspectors, or utility crews cannot reasonably reach the site, officials have a very good reason to say no.

Septic and water issues can also signal a dead end. If the lot is too small for a code-compliant septic system, lacks approved soil conditions, or cannot secure a lawful water source, the property may never support a full-time residence. That is especially true in rural areas where people assume off-grid living automatically solves the problem. Off-grid can work in some places, but it does not erase health department rules. If the local agency has already said the parcel cannot support sanitation for another dwelling, or if the site has known soil, drainage, or setback conflicts, do not assume you can "design around" it.

Be cautious when officials keep giving you vague answers like "maybe," "it depends," or "we usually don't allow that." Sometimes that means there is a real path and they just want a better application. But if every office you talk to sounds uncertain, unhelpful, or quietly negative, that can be a sign the location is outside the normal legal framework. Tiny-house projects need some combination of clear rules, existing permit categories, or a history of similar approvals. If no one can point to a path that has actually worked before, you may be trying to force a one-off exception in a place that does not want one.

Another bad sign is when the property depends on a chain of approvals that all have to go perfectly, and none of them are guaranteed. For example, maybe the zoning office might consider the use, the building department might accept the structure, the health department might approve septic, the utility company might approve service, and the HOA might still object. If the project only works if five different gatekeepers all feel generous at the same time, that is not a solid plan. The more approvals you need, the more likely one of them will fail and take the whole project down with it.

Watch out for land that is marketed with a lot of cheerful language but very little legal detail. Phrases like “tiny-house friendly,” “perfect for off-grid living,” or “great for your dream cabin” do not mean much unless they are backed by actual approvals, zoning language, and site facts. If the seller cannot tell you the zoning district, the permitted uses, the utility status, the septic history, or whether similar dwellings have ever been approved there, treat that silence as information. A property that is truly workable usually has a paper trail. A property that only sounds workable in a listing often does not.

Finally, trust your own frustration level. If every answer feels like a workaround, every approval sounds conditional, and every official conversation ends with a new obstacle, the site may simply not be the right one. Tiny-house legality is hard enough when the location is cooperating. When the property itself keeps sending the message that it does not want a dwelling there, believe it. The cheapest and least painful legal strategy is often the one that starts with a better parcel.

Chapter 8: Working With Officials Without Losing Your Mind

Once you get past the paperwork and into the actual conversation with the people who review, interpret, and sometimes enforce the rules, tiny-house projects become less about forms and more about communication. That is where a lot of good plans get slowed down for reasons that have nothing to do with the house itself. A vague answer can send you in circles. A rushed answer can cost you weeks. A defensive tone can turn a simple clarification into a turf war nobody needed. The good news is that officials usually respond better when the exchange feels organized, specific, and respectful, even if the answer is not the one you hoped for.

How to ask the right questions and get them answered in writing

The fastest way to get a useful answer from a planning office, building department, or code official is to stop asking broad, fuzzy questions. “Can I build a tiny house here?” is almost guaranteed to get you a vague answer, a shrug, or a referral to someone else. Officials can only answer well when you give them a specific fact pattern: the parcel, the zoning district, the kind of structure, whether it is on wheels or a foundation, whether it will be occupied full-time, and whether you are asking about building approval, land use approval, or both. The more precise your question, the less room there is for everyone to talk past each other.

A good question usually has three parts: what the property is, what the structure is, and what use you want. For example: "I own Parcel 14-22-08 in the R-1 district. I want to place a 320-square-foot tiny house on a permanent foundation as a second dwelling behind an existing single-family home. Can you tell me whether that use is allowed, and if so, what permits would be required?" That question gives the office something real to work with. It is also much harder for them to answer with a meaningless "tiny houses aren't allowed" statement, because you have forced the issue into the actual code categories that matter.

It helps to ask one issue at a time instead of dumping your whole project on the first person who answers the phone. Zoning, building code, utilities, septic, driveway access, and occupancy can all involve different reviewers. If you ask six questions at once, you may get six half-answers back. Start with the gatekeeping question: is the proposed use allowed on this parcel? If the answer is yes, move to the next layer: what structure type is acceptable, what permits are needed, and what documents should be submitted. If the answer is no, ask whether there is a different category, exception, or permit path that could work. That keeps the conversation organized and makes it easier to document.

When you talk to officials, write down the name, title, department, date, and exact wording of the answer as soon as the conversation ends. Better yet, follow up by email the same day and politely confirm your understanding. A short message is usually enough: "Thank you for speaking with me today. I want to make sure I understood your guidance correctly. You indicated that a tiny house on a permanent foundation may be considered an accessory dwelling unit in this district, subject to site plan review and building permit approval. Please let me know if that is inaccurate." This kind of email does two things. It creates a paper trail, and it gives the official a chance to correct any misunderstanding before you rely on the answer.

Getting answers in writing matters because memory is slippery and office opinions can change. The person you speak with today may not be the person reviewing your permit next month. A verbal “sure, that sounds fine” is comforting, but it is not much protection if the next reviewer says the first person was mistaken. Written responses do not always create a binding legal promise, but they do give you something concrete to point to if the project gets questioned later. Even a simple email response can be useful if it clearly identifies the property, the proposal, and the department’s position.

Be careful about the difference between an informal opinion and an official determination. Some staff will happily tell you what they think over the phone, but that is not always the same as a formal ruling. If the issue is important, ask whether the answer is being given as general guidance or as an official interpretation of the code for your parcel. If the department has a formal review process, use it. If there is a zoning clearance letter, pre-application review, or written code interpretation request, that paper may be worth far more than a hallway conversation. It is also smarter to ask for the specific code section or ordinance language behind the answer, because that lets you verify what they are relying on instead of guessing.

There are a few questions that tend to get better results than others. Try asking:

What zoning district applies to this parcel, and what residential uses are allowed there?

Would a tiny house on wheels be treated differently from a tiny house on a foundation?

If this is intended as an accessory dwelling unit, what size, setback, parking, or owner-occupancy rules apply?

Which department handles the first approval step, and what documents do you need to see before issuing a decision?

Is there a written policy, ordinance, or code section that supports that answer?

What you want to avoid is sounding like you are asking for permission to ignore the rules. Officials are much more responsive when the tone is calm, specific, and respectful. You are not trying to win an argument on the spot. You are trying to build a record that shows you asked clear questions and received clear answers. If the answer is uncertain, that is useful too, because it tells you where the real problem is and whether you need a planner, designer, engineer, or attorney to help decode it before you spend money. The goal is not to get the answer you hope for. The goal is to get the answer that will still be there when your plans, permit packet, and future move-in date depend on it.

Building a respectful relationship with local officials

Local officials are a lot easier to work with when you stop treating them like gatekeepers and start treating them like people who have a job to do. That does not mean you have to agree with every rule or pretend the process is painless. It means you get farther when you show up prepared, respectful, and specific. A planning clerk, zoning administrator, or building inspector is more likely to help you untangle a tiny-house question when you are calm, organized, and not asking them to solve your whole life in one phone call. They are usually dealing with a steady stream of confused, frustrated, or overly ambitious people. If you can be the person who makes the conversation easier instead of harder, you immediately stand out in a good way.

Respect starts with understanding the pressure they are under. Officials are not just thinking about your tiny house; they are thinking about consistency, fairness, liability, public safety, and whether their answer will hold up if someone complains later. That is why a friendly "Can you just tell me if tiny houses are allowed?" often goes nowhere. A better approach is to give them the facts they need to answer the question they are actually responsible for answering. For example, you might say the parcel address, the zoning district, whether the unit is on wheels or a foundation, whether it will be occupied full-time, and whether you are asking about a primary dwelling, accessory dwelling unit, or temporary setup. The more clearly you frame the issue, the less likely you are to get a vague answer that sends you back to square one.

It also helps to remember that different offices have different lanes. The planning department may care about land use and setbacks, while the building department cares about construction and life-safety details, and the utility or health department may have their own concerns about septic, water, or sanitation. If you walk into one office expecting a complete answer to every part of the project, you may leave disappointed. Instead, treat the process like a guided tour through separate pieces of the system. Be polite about asking who handles what, and do not act like someone is being difficult just because they cannot answer a question that belongs to another department. That attitude alone can keep a conversation from turning defensive.

One of the simplest ways to build trust is to keep your requests small and concrete. Rather than asking, "Can I live in a tiny house here?" ask, "Is this parcel eligible for an accessory dwelling unit if the primary home already exists?" Or, "Does your code treat a tiny house on a foundation as a single-family dwelling if it meets residential standards?" Or, "What documents do you need to review whether a tiny house on wheels can be approved as an accessory structure?" Questions like these show that you have done enough homework to be taken seriously. They also make it easier for the official to give you an answer that is actually useful instead of a general warning.

Written communication matters just as much as the tone of the conversation. If an official gives you helpful guidance by phone or in person, follow up with a short email that says what you understood and asks them to confirm or correct it. That is not being pushy; it is protecting both sides from misunderstandings. A message like, "Thank you for speaking with me today. My understanding is that a tiny house on a permanent foundation may be reviewed as a dwelling in this district, but a wheeled unit would need separate approval. Please let me know if I misunderstood," gives them a clean chance to clarify. It also creates a paper trail, which is useful if your project gets passed from one staff member to another.

There is also a difference between being respectful and being passive. You can be courteous without acting like you have no right to ask follow-up questions. If the first answer is unclear, ask for the code section, ordinance number, or policy that supports it. If someone says, "We usually do not allow that," ask what "usually" means in practice. If they tell you a tiny house is not allowed, ask whether the problem is zoning, building code, utility access, or a private restriction. That kind of follow-up is not combative. It is how you avoid building your whole plan on a half-answer. Officials often appreciate it when you are trying to understand the rule instead of trying to argue your way around it.

What you want to avoid is the temptation to lead with frustration. Tiny-house advocates have good reasons to feel tired, especially after hearing inconsistent answers from different offices. But if you walk in sounding like the system is stupid, unfair, or out to get you, the conversation can harden fast. Even when you are right on the merits, a hostile tone can make people less willing to help you troubleshoot. A better strategy is to stay firm about your goal and flexible about the path.

You do not have to hide your enthusiasm, but pair it with enough professionalism that the official can see you are serious, organized, and likely to follow through.

Over time, the best relationships with local officials are built the same way good tiny-house projects are built: one careful step at a time. Show up with the facts. Ask for clarity. Confirm what you heard. Be patient when the answer is "I need to check." And when someone takes the time to help, acknowledge it. That kind of interaction does not guarantee approval, but it does make the process less adversarial. In a world where tiny-house rules can be murky, a respectful working relationship may be the difference between getting bounced around and getting a real path forward.

What to do when the rules seem vague or contradictory

When the rules start sounding fuzzy, the first move is not to guess your way through them. It is to slow down and figure out whether the problem is actually vagueness, or whether you are looking at two different rules that apply to two different parts of the project. A lot of tiny-house confusion comes from people asking one question and getting an answer that quietly depends on another one. "Can I build this?" may trigger a building-code response, while "Can I live in this here?" triggers zoning, and "Can I park this on my lot?" may lead to a third answer entirely. If the language feels slippery, break the issue into pieces: use, structure, location, occupancy, and duration. That alone clears up a surprising amount of the fog.

The next step is to pin everything to the exact source. If someone says, "That is not allowed," ask what rule they are relying on and where it lives. A code section, ordinance number, zoning district table, or written policy memo is much more useful than a verbal "we usually don't do that." Tiny-house projects often get stalled by office habits, not just written law. One person may be repeating an old interpretation, another may be thinking of a different district, and a third may be trying to be helpful without actually committing the department to anything. You do not need to argue in the hallway. You need a citation, a date, and ideally an email or letter that shows exactly what was said.

Once you have the source, read it like someone who expects a trap, because sometimes there is one. Vague rules often hide in words like "adequate," "suitable," "permanent," "habitable," "detached," "temporary," or "customary." Those words can be legal gold mines or legal landmines depending on how the local government uses them. If a rule says a dwelling must be "permanent," ask what counts as permanent in that jurisdiction. If it says a unit must be "customary," ask customary for which neighborhood, zoning district, or housing type. If the code does not define the term, that does not mean anything goes. It means the decision may depend on local interpretation, which is exactly why written clarification matters so much.

Contradictions usually show up in one of three ways. Sometimes one rule is broader and another is more specific, and the specific rule wins. Sometimes a newer ordinance quietly changed the older one, but nobody has updated the website or the handout. And sometimes different departments are reading the same language through different lenses. Planning may be focused on land use, building may be focused on safety, and utilities may be focused on service capacity. If a zoning table seems to allow a tiny house but a building official seems skeptical, do not assume one office is wrong and the other is right. Ask how the departments coordinate and which approval comes first. A project can be technically allowed in one sense and still be impossible in another if the steps are out of order.

This is where the "show me the path" question becomes useful. Instead of asking, "Is this okay?" ask, "What would make this approvable here?" That phrasing is less confrontational and more productive. It invites the official to explain the missing piece rather than defend a flat yes or no. Maybe the issue is lot size. Maybe it is foundation design. Maybe the structure is allowed only as an accessory dwelling unit, not as a primary residence. Maybe the lot needs a variance, a special permit, or a different utility plan. If the answer is still unclear, ask for the minimum change that would move the project forward. Sometimes a tiny adjustment in classification, siting, or paperwork solves what sounded like a hard no.

It also helps to watch for unofficial answers that sound confident but are not actually reliable. "We've never approved one like that," is not the same as "the code prohibits it." "The inspector won't like it," is not the same as "it fails the code." "That's how we've always done it," is not the same as a written rule. In tiny-house work, people often get discouraged by attitude before they ever hit a true legal barrier. That is why written records matter. If the office will not email an answer, send a polite follow-up summarizing the conversation and asking them to confirm or correct it. You are not being difficult. You are building a paper trail that protects you if the story changes later.

When the rules still seem contradictory after you have the text in front of you, look for the decision-maker, not just the desk you happened to visit. Some offices can explain the rule but cannot interpret gray areas. Some staff can point you to the right section but cannot tell you how they will apply it to your parcel. If the issue is important enough, ask whether there is a supervisor, zoning administrator, building official, or planning director who can review the question. You are not trying to climb the ladder out of impatience. You are trying to make sure the answer comes from someone with authority to stand behind it. That matters a lot more than getting a quick reply from the first person who answers the phone.

And if the contradiction really is baked into the system, do not rush to force a clean answer where none exists. Sometimes the best move is to choose the rule path that is most defensible and narrow the project to fit it. Other times the better move is to wait for a formal interpretation, variance, or amendment process rather than betting your money on a loose reading. Tiny-house projects do not usually fail because the law was crystal clear and the owner ignored it. They fail because someone treated uncertainty like permission. When the language is murky, your job is not to become a legal theorist. Your job is to turn uncertainty into something written, specific, and reviewable before you spend real money on the wrong version of the dream.

How to advocate for your project without sounding combative

The fastest way to lose an official is to sound like you are trying to win an argument instead of solve a problem. Tiny-house projects can make people defensive fast, especially if the local office has already heard a lot of "But this should be allowed" speeches. If you walk in acting like the rules are foolish, outdated, or optional, you are basically asking the person across the counter to protect the system by saying no. A better approach is to frame your project as something you want to do the right way, with their help, under the rules that actually apply. That does not mean being fake or overly polite. It means making it easier for them to see you as a prepared applicant instead of a nuisance.

Start by separating your frustration from your question. You may feel like the zoning code is absurd, the setback rule is arbitrary, or the minimum size requirement makes no sense for a tiny house. Fine. You can think all of that privately. But when you speak to staff, lead with the narrow issue you need answered. "I'm trying to determine whether a tiny house on a foundation can be approved as an accessory dwelling unit on this parcel" is a working question. "Your rules make no sense and tiny houses are the future" is a conversation killer. Officials usually respond better when you show that you understand they are working inside a system, not inventing obstacles out of spite.

One of the best habits you can build is to make your language match the department's language. If the code talks about a "dwelling unit," use that phrase. If the office distinguishes between a "primary structure" and an "accessory structure," use those terms instead of your own shorthand. If you keep saying "my tiny home" when the issue is really whether the structure qualifies as an "accessory dwelling unit," you may accidentally make your project sound less clear than it is. This is not about being stiff. It is about showing that you have done enough homework to have a real conversation. People are much more willing to help when they do not have to translate your entire request before they can answer it.

It also helps to ask for the decision path, not just the decision. If you want to know whether a project is possible, do not only ask yes-or-no questions. Ask what information the office needs to evaluate it, which department will review it, and what the likely next step would be if the answer is maybe instead of yes. That keeps the conversation practical. It also prevents you from sounding like you are trying to corner someone into an on-the-spot approval. A planner or code official is often more comfortable saying, "Here is what we would need to see," than making a broad promise about a project they have not reviewed. When you invite them to explain the process, you make it easier for them to stay helpful.

Another useful move is to show that you are not asking them to ignore the rules, only to help you understand how the rules apply. That distinction matters. Officials hear a lot of disguised requests for special treatment. If your tone suggests you want an exception before you have even established the basic facts, you may get resistance. But if you say something like, "I want to make sure I'm reading this correctly before I invest in plans," you come across as responsible. You are not challenging their authority. You are trying to avoid wasting everyone's time. That is a much easier posture for them to respond to.

When the answer is not what you hoped for, resist the urge to debate immediately. A lot of tiny-house advocates accidentally turn a simple clarification into a showdown by reacting too fast. Instead of arguing the first time you hear "no," ask what part of the code is driving the answer and whether there is another path that might fit. Sometimes the issue is not the whole project, just one detail: lot size, foundation type, occupancy status, utility access, or a missing document. If you push too hard too soon, you may never get to the real issue. Calm follow-up questions sound far more professional than trying to out-talk the person who controls the permit file.

It can also help to make your project easy to support on paper. Bring a short written summary, a site address or parcel number, and a few specific facts: whether the unit is on wheels or a foundation, whether it will be occupied full-time, and what kind of approval you are seeking. If you have already checked the zoning district and private restrictions, say so. If you are still unsure, say that too. Officials are usually more comfortable with a person who admits uncertainty than with someone who sounds certain but is clearly missing key information. Being honest about what you know and what you still need is not weakness. It is how you avoid sounding combative while still advocating for yourself.

Finally, remember that being respectful does not mean being passive. You can be firm without being hostile. You can disagree without sounding like you are accusing someone of blocking your dream on purpose. The goal is not to shrink your position until it disappears. The goal is to present it in a way that keeps the door open. If you stay specific, calm, and solution-focused, you give officials a reason to help you move the project forward instead of a reason to defend the first no that comes to mind.

Chapter 9: Special Situations and Real-World Workarounds

Not every tiny-house problem fits neatly into the usual zoning-and-code conversation. Some projects live in the spaces where the rules get murky, the exceptions get narrow, and the official answer depends on a few very specific facts about the site and the way the home will be used. That is where people start looking for workable paths instead of perfect ones. The next few sections stay in that territory: the places where tiny-house owners try to make a legal life out of systems that were not always designed with them in mind.

Off-grid power, composting toilets, and alternative systems

Off-grid systems are one of those tiny-house topics that sound wonderfully simple until you try to make them legal. A solar panel on the roof, a battery bank in the corner, a composting toilet in the bathroom, maybe a rainwater setup outside, and suddenly you are not just building a small home. You are asking the local government to accept a whole alternative infrastructure package. Some places are fine with that. Others are deeply suspicious of it. The legal question is rarely whether the system works in the real world. It is whether the system satisfies the local rules for sanitation, utility access, and habitability.

Power is usually the easiest place to start, but even there, "off-grid" does not always mean "no rules." A solar setup may be allowed, but the electrical system still has to be installed safely and may still need permits and inspections. If the house is going to be occupied full-time, officials may want to know how backup power works, how the batteries are housed, and whether the system was designed by someone who understands the code. In some jurisdictions, the issue is not the source of power but the expectation that a dwelling be connected to an approved utility system or at least capable of meeting local safety standards. A beautiful off-grid setup can still get stuck if the building department sees it as incomplete, improvised, or too far outside the normal residential model.

Water and wastewater tend to cause even more trouble than electricity. A tiny house on a rural parcel may be perfectly fine with a well and septic system, but those systems usually require separate permits, soil testing, and site approval. If the lot cannot support a septic field, the whole project may be dead unless the local rules allow some other approved method. That is where composting toilets, graywater systems, and water storage tanks enter the picture. The problem is that these alternatives are not universally recognized. Some places treat them as acceptable if they are installed and maintained properly. Others only allow them in very limited circumstances, or not at all for permanent residence. So the question is not "Does the toilet work?" It is "Does this county accept this toilet as a lawful sanitation solution for a dwelling on this parcel?"

Composting toilets are a perfect example of the gap between practical use and legal acceptance. Many tiny-house owners love them because they save water, reduce infrastructure needs, and fit compact designs. But a composting toilet does not automatically satisfy a local health department just because it is marketed as eco-friendly. Some jurisdictions require a conventional septic system for any occupied residence. Others will allow a composting toilet only if the home also has a permitted graywater system, a certain number of plumbing fixtures, or a plan for waste handling that meets public health requirements. In a few places, the code may be silent or outdated, which sounds promising until you realize silence often means the official has to decide whether to approve it case by case. That can go either way depending on who is reviewing the file and how comfortable they are with alternative systems.

It also matters whether the tiny house is meant to be temporary, seasonal, or permanent. A composting toilet that might be tolerated in a cabin used on weekends can become a bigger issue when the same setup is part of a full-time residence. The same goes for water storage. A tank and delivery system may be acceptable for short-term use, a rural retreat, or an emergency shelter arrangement, but not for a permanent home that is supposed to meet local dwelling standards. Officials are often less concerned with whether you can personally live that way and more concerned with whether the arrangement creates sanitation risks, nuisance issues, or a precedent they do not want to set for the rest of the area.

Alternative systems can also trigger a chain reaction in other parts of the code. If you are off-grid for power, water, and sewer, the local office may start asking how the house handles heating, cooking, fire safety, access for emergency responders, and year-round occupancy. A project that looks self-sufficient from the outside may be treated as under-served or incomplete from the code's point of view. That is especially true if the home is on wheels or built in a way that does not fit neatly into the ordinary residential categories. The more your setup departs from standard utility connections, the more important it becomes to show that each alternative system is recognized, permitted if necessary, and installed in a way that does not create a safety problem.

If you want to pursue off-grid systems without getting blindsided, the smartest move is to separate three questions: is the system technically workable, is it permitted by the local rules, and is it acceptable for the specific use you want? Those are not the same question. A solar array may be legal on the property but still need an electrical permit. A composting toilet may be environmentally sound but not satisfy the health department for permanent occupancy. A rainwater system may be allowed for irrigation or emergency backup but not as the primary potable water source without treatment and approval. Tiny-house owners get into trouble when they assume one green feature automatically unlocks the whole package. In practice, each system has to stand on its own and also fit into the larger legal story of the property.

That is why it helps to ask officials about alternative systems before the build is too far along. Once the house is finished, it is much harder to change the plumbing, reroute the electrical setup, or redesign the sanitation plan just to satisfy a rule you did not check early enough. For off-grid living, the legal win usually comes from matching the system to the property and documenting it well, not from hoping the inspector will admire your independence and let the details slide.

Temporary living arrangements during construction or emergencies

Temporary housing sounds like a side issue until it becomes the whole project. If your tiny house is still under construction, or your normal home suddenly becomes unlivable because of fire, flood, storm damage, or a major repair, the question shifts from "Can I live tiny here forever?" to "Can I legally stay somewhere right now?" That is a different legal conversation. Local officials may be more flexible in a true emergency, but they usually still care about sanitation, access, safety, and how long the arrangement will last. A temporary setup is often tolerated because it is temporary, not because it is automatically approved.

For people building a tiny house on their own property, the most common temporary arrangement is staying in the existing main house, a garage apartment, an RV, a travel trailer, or another structure while the new unit is being built. Whether that is allowed depends on the zoning district, the occupancy rules, and sometimes the building department's view of what counts as a legitimate construction period. Some places allow a homeowner to live in a trailer or RV on-site while building a permitted house, but only for a limited time and only after getting a specific permit or written approval. Others allow the temporary setup only if there is an active construction permit and visible progress. If the project stalls, the temporary permission can disappear.

That "temporary" label matters a lot more than people expect. A zoning office may be willing to approve a hardship situation or a temporary occupancy permit for a set number of days or months, but that approval usually comes with conditions. You may need proof that the permanent dwelling is under permit review or under construction. You may need a septic approval, a water source, or a safe way for emergency vehicles to reach the site. You may also be limited to one temporary unit on the lot, and you may be prohibited from renting it out or adding extra occupants. In other words, the government is often saying, "We will tolerate this while you finish the real plan," not, "We have reclassified your property as a tiny-house-friendly campground."

Emergency housing works a little differently, but the same basic caution applies. After a disaster, local governments sometimes relax enforcement or create emergency shelter rules that let people use RVs, mobile homes, tiny houses on wheels, or other temporary structures while repairs are underway. Those emergency permissions can come from a city council action, a county emergency order, a state disaster declaration, or a building official exercising limited discretion. But they are usually tied to the disaster itself and to a specific time window. If you assume an emergency allowance has become a permanent right, you can end up with a violation notice once the emergency period ends.

It also helps to separate the structure from the use. A tiny house on wheels may be physically suitable as temporary shelter, but that does not mean the zoning code sees it that way. The same unit might be acceptable as a construction trailer, disaster-relief shelter, or temporary guest unit, yet still not qualify as a dwelling that can be occupied full-time on that parcel. Officials often care less about the romance of the setup and more about whether the arrangement creates a legal residence, a short-term occupancy, or an accessory use tied to a current permit. If you are asking for temporary living rights, be ready to explain exactly who will live there, for how long, and under what permit or emergency authority.

Sanitation is usually the make-or-break issue. Even when a local office is willing to allow temporary occupancy, it may still require approved wastewater disposal, potable water, and a safe electrical connection. A composting toilet or off-grid setup may be fine in one county and a hard no in another, especially if the temporary unit is being used as a residence rather than a jobsite shelter. If you are staying in an RV or tiny house during construction, do not assume a hose, a generator, and a portable toilet will satisfy the inspector. Temporary living arrangements often get approved only when the site can function like a safe, minimal home, not just a place to sleep.

The best move is to ask for the temporary rule in writing before anyone moves in. Use plain language and give the official the exact facts: the parcel address, the existing zoning, the structure you want to use, whether the unit is on wheels or a foundation, the reason for the temporary stay, and the expected end date. If there is an emergency declaration, include that too. Then ask the direct question: what permit, waiver, or written approval is required for temporary occupancy, and what conditions apply? That question forces the office to identify the legal path instead of giving you a casual answer that turns out to mean something narrower later.

One last trap: a temporary living arrangement can quietly become permanent if nobody tracks the deadline. That is where people get into trouble. The permit expires, the emergency order ends, the construction drags on, and suddenly the "short-term" setup has been on the lot long enough to attract enforcement. If you are relying on a temporary arrangement, treat the expiration date like a real legal deadline, not a suggestion. Keep copies of the approval, note the renewal rules, and do not assume that being in the middle of a project gives you unlimited extra time. In tiny-house law, temporary permission is still permission with an end point.

Rural properties, agricultural exemptions, and unincorporated areas

Rural land can feel like the easiest place to put a tiny house, and sometimes it is. There is often more space, fewer neighbors to complain, and a local culture that is less interested in how your home looks from the road. But "rural" does not mean "rule-free," and that is where people get tripped up. A parcel being outside city limits does not automatically make it legal to place any kind of dwelling on it. The county may still have zoning rules, minimum lot sizes, setback requirements, driveway standards, utility requirements, floodplain limits, or health department rules that control exactly what can happen there. In other words, the land may look open, but the legal map can still be full of lines.

One of the biggest differences in rural areas is that the county often becomes the main decision-maker. If the property is in an unincorporated area, there may be no city zoning office at all, which sounds convenient until you realize the county's rules may be broader, stricter, or just harder to find. Some counties regulate land use lightly. Others have very specific ordinances for dwellings, agricultural structures, manufactured homes, RVs, and accessory units. If you are assuming that unincorporated means relaxed, you can end up with a very expensive surprise. The first question is not "Is this rural?" It is "Which government actually controls this parcel, and what category of use does it allow here?"

Agricultural zoning can be especially tempting for tiny-house fans because it seems to promise flexibility. That flexibility is real in some places, but it is usually tied to the land's farming purpose, not to a general freedom to live however you want. Many agricultural zones are designed to protect farmland, support farm operations, and keep non-farm development from crowding out agricultural use. That can work in your favor if your tiny house is part of a legitimate farm operation, housing for farm labor, a caretaker dwelling, or a permitted accessory use. But if the parcel is simply zoned agricultural and you want to place a tiny house there as a full-time residence with no farm connection, the code may still say no or may require a special permit, a second dwelling approval, or proof that the use fits the agricultural purpose.

That distinction matters because "agricultural exemption" is a phrase people use loosely, and it can mean very different things depending on the context. Sometimes it refers to a zoning exemption or reduced regulation for farm-related structures. Sometimes it refers to tax treatment. Sometimes it refers to a building-code exception for certain farm buildings that are not intended as dwellings. None of those automatically gives you a legal right to live in a tiny house on the land. A barn is not a bedroom. A shed is not a residence just because it sits on acreage. And a property getting an agricultural tax break does not mean the county has waived its housing rules.

If your tiny house is going onto land with a farm use, the local government may ask whether it is actually part of the agricultural operation or whether it is just a house in disguise. That can affect everything from occupancy approval to septic sizing to whether the structure needs full residential code compliance. Some counties are comfortable with a dwelling on agricultural land if the parcel is large enough and the use is clearly tied to the property's function. Others are wary of people using agricultural zoning as a loophole for suburban-style residential development. If the code uses terms like "farm dwelling," "agricultural employee housing," "caretaker unit," or "temporary farm accommodation," those words matter a lot. They are not decorative. They are the boundaries of what the county thinks is allowed.

Unincorporated areas can also create a false sense of freedom because the rules may be less visible, not because they are less real. In a city, you can usually find zoning maps, permit portals, and a building department that deals with residential questions all day. In a rural county, the process may be spread across planning, environmental health, public works, and the assessor's office. One office may care about the septic system, another about the driveway and emergency access, another about whether the structure counts as a dwelling, and another about whether the parcel can support a second residence. If you only ask one department, you may get an answer that is technically true but incomplete.

That is why rural tiny-house projects work best when you stop relying on assumptions about "country property" and start checking the actual use rules for the parcel. Look for the permitted uses in that zoning district, any limits on dwellings per acre, and any special rules for farm-related housing. Ask whether the county treats tiny houses on foundations differently from movable units, and whether an accessory dwelling unit is allowed outside city limits. If the land is in a rural subdivision, don't forget private restrictions either. Rural does not always mean unrestricted. A deed covenant can be just as effective in the middle of nowhere as it is in a suburban neighborhood.

For tiny-house owners, the cleanest rural path is usually the one where the land use and the house category match each other instead of fighting. A tiny house intended as a permanent dwelling is easier to defend when the parcel already allows a residence. A tiny house tied to a real agricultural use is easier to justify when the county recognizes that type of occupancy. And a parcel in an unincorporated area is easiest to work with when you have written confirmation from the county about what it will and will not approve. Rural land can absolutely be a good fit for tiny living, but the legal advantage comes from the right facts, not from the scenery.

Short-term rentals, guest houses, and other gray areas

Short-term rentals, guest houses, and similar setups live in a weird middle zone where tiny-house rules can get especially slippery. A lot of the time, the structure itself is not the main problem. The problem is the use. A tiny house that might be hard to approve as a full-time residence can sometimes be easier to permit as a guest house, accessory unit, or temporary rental. But the reverse is also true: a structure that would be tolerated as a secondary space can become a zoning problem the moment money changes hands or someone starts sleeping there every weekend.

That is why the first question is usually not "Can I build a tiny house here?" but "What is this thing going to be used for?" Local governments often care a lot more about occupancy pattern than about charm, square footage, or even whether the place looks permanent. A backyard tiny house used by family members may be treated as an accessory structure or an ADU, depending on the code. The same unit listed on a rental platform for two-night stays may trigger a completely different set of rules. Some towns regulate short-term rentals through zoning. Others use business licensing, occupancy limits, nuisance rules, or local tax registration. In a few places, all of those layers show up at once.

Guest houses are another area where the label can help or hurt you. In some jurisdictions, a guest house is allowed only if it is clearly subordinate to a primary residence and not rented separately. That means no full kitchen in some places, no separate address in others, and sometimes no independent utilities or mailbox. The local code may allow a "guest suite" but not a separate dwelling unit. If you add features that make the space function like its own home, officials may decide you have crossed the line from guest use into a second dwelling. That can matter a lot if the lot is only allowed to hold one residence.

Short-term rentals create their own set of headaches because the law often treats them less like housing and more like a commercial activity. Even if the tiny house is physically allowed on the lot, renting it out by the night can trigger rules about transient lodging, hotel taxes, fire safety, parking, neighborhood compatibility, and owner presence. Some cities require the owner to live on-site. Some require a local contact person. Some ban short-term rentals outright in certain zoning districts. If your plan is to use a tiny house as an income property, you need to know whether the local code sees that as residential use, lodging use, or something in between. Those categories are not interchangeable.

This is where people get into trouble by assuming that "if it is legal to live in, it must be legal to rent." Not necessarily. A tiny house can be perfectly acceptable as an ADU for a relative and still be prohibited as a vacation rental. Or it may be allowed as a short-term rental only if it meets fire code requirements that are stricter than what applies to ordinary private occupancy. In some places, the structure also has to be inspected or registered as a rental unit before it can be advertised. Skipping that step can turn a clever side hustle into a code enforcement problem very fast.

Another gray area is the line between a guest house and an independent dwelling. The more your tiny house can function on its own, the more likely officials are to treat it as a separate unit. That usually means a private bathroom, a full kitchen, dedicated sleeping space, and independent access. If the zoning only permits one dwelling on the lot, those features can be read as evidence that you have created a second residence, even if you call it a studio, casita, or backyard retreat. The name on the listing matters less than how the space actually operates.

If you are trying to fit into one of these gray zones, the safest move is to get very specific about use and get the answer in writing. Ask whether the structure may be used as a guest house, an ADU, or a short-term rental in the exact zoning district where the property sits. Ask whether owner occupancy is required. Ask whether the unit needs a separate permit, business license, or tax registration. Ask whether the rules change if the unit is on wheels, on a foundation, or attached to utilities. The more you can pin the official down on the actual use, the less likely you are to build something that looks fine on paper but gets flagged later.

It also helps to remember that "temporary" is not a magic word. A lot of tiny-house owners tell themselves that if the rental is occasional, seasonal, or just for a few months, the rules will be looser. Sometimes they are. But often the code defines short-term occupancy by the length of stay, not by how casual the arrangement feels to you. A place that is rented for less than 30 days, or less than 14 days, or more than a certain number of times per year may fall into a special category whether you intended it or not. In gray-area situations, the calendar can matter just as much as the floor plan.

Chapter 10: How to Build a Tiny House Legal Strategy

Once you stop asking only whether a tiny house is "possible" and start asking how to make it legally survivable from start to finish, the whole project gets clearer. That shift matters because tiny-house plans usually fail at the seams, not in one dramatic place: a missed permit, a bad assumption about the lot, an expensive professional you did not realize you needed, or a build choice that quietly closes off your best legal path. This next part is about turning scattered decisions into a workable strategy so you are not improvising every time a rule shows up.

Creating your personal legal checklist

The best legal checklist for a tiny house is not a giant binder of everything that might matter. It is a short, ruthless list of the things that can actually stop your project. Start by separating the "nice to know" questions from the "must know before spending money" questions. If you are still at the dreaming stage, your checklist should focus on the parcel, the legal category of the structure, and the approvals required to put it there. If you already own land, the checklist should shift toward zoning, setbacks, utilities, and whether the structure you want can be approved as a dwelling, an accessory unit, or something else entirely. The point is to make the law concrete enough that you can compare one real option against another instead of wandering through a pile of vague advice.

A good personal checklist usually starts with the property itself. Ask: Who controls this land? What is the zoning district? What uses are allowed by right, and what uses need special approval? Are there deed restrictions, HOA rules, or private covenants that could block the plan even if the city is fine with it? What is the minimum lot size, and is there already a primary dwelling on the parcel? If you are considering a tiny house on wheels, does the local government treat it like a dwelling, an RV, a trailer, or something in between? If you are considering a foundation-built tiny house, does the code path require a full residential permit, an ADU permit, or a manufactured housing approval? Those questions do not sound glamorous, but they are the ones that tell you whether the rest of the project is worth pursuing.

Next, put the structure itself on the checklist in plain language. Do not just write “tiny house.” Write the version you are actually proposing: on wheels or on a foundation, full-time residence or occasional use, primary home or accessory unit, off-grid or connected to utilities. Then list the technical features that could matter to a reviewer: sleeping loft, loft ladder or stair, composting toilet, propane appliances, solar power, water storage, septic connection, and emergency exits. You do not need to become a code expert overnight, but you do need to know which features are likely to trigger extra questions. A tiny house with a loft and a compact stair may be perfectly normal in tiny-house culture and still raise code issues if the local rules expect standard ceiling heights, stair dimensions, or egress windows. Your checklist should flag those issues early, before they become expensive redesigns.

After that, build a permit and approval line item for each step you expect to face. A lot of people make the mistake of thinking “permit” is one thing. It is usually several things. You may need zoning approval first, then a building permit, then utility approval, then septic or water sign-off, then inspections, then a certificate of occupancy or some other final authorization. If your project is on a tight timeline, add estimated lead times next to each step. That way you can see where the real bottleneck is. For example, a parcel might be zoned correctly, but if the county requires a septic design before it will even review the dwelling permit, that becomes the pacing item. Your checklist should show the order of operations, not just the names of the forms.

It also helps to include a "proof" column. Tiny-house legality often turns on what you can show, not just what you believe. For each issue on your checklist, note the document that proves the answer. That might be a zoning letter, a printed ordinance section, an email from planning staff, a site plan, a survey, a deed, a covenant, or a permit application receipt. If an official tells you something important over the phone, write down the date, the name, and the department, then follow up by email if you can. The goal is not to create a legal drama file. The goal is to avoid building your whole plan on a memory. When the rules are unclear, written confirmation is worth a lot more than a friendly verbal "sure, probably."

Money belongs on the checklist too, because legal feasibility and financial feasibility are not separate questions. Add estimates for permit fees, impact fees, plan review costs, survey work, engineering, septic design, utility connection charges, and any professional help you may need. If you are trying to live in a tiny house cheaply, it is especially important to know what the legal path costs before you commit. A low-cost build can become a high-cost project if the site needs grading, the county wants stamped drawings, or the zoning board requires a hearing. Put those possible costs in the checklist as line items, even if they are only rough estimates. That gives you a more honest picture of whether the project is still within reach.

Finally, add a simple decision rule to the end of your checklist: what would make you move forward, pause, or walk away? That might sound overly formal, but it keeps you from drifting into wishful thinking. For example, you might decide that you will move ahead only if the zoning allows the use, the structure can be approved under the local code path, and the utility situation can be solved without a major variance. If one of those pieces is missing, you pause and gather more information. If two or more are missing, you walk away and look for a different parcel or a different legal category. That kind of rule is not about being pessimistic. It is about protecting your time, your money, and your enthusiasm from a project that looks good until the paperwork catches up with it.

If you want the checklist to stay useful, keep it short enough that you will actually use it. A one-page checklist with notes is better than a twenty-page packet nobody opens. The real value comes from updating it every time you learn something new. Tiny-house law changes fast, and local offices do not always explain things the same way from one week to the next. A living checklist gives you a place to sort the facts, track the questions, and see where the project stands without pretending the path is clearer than it really is.

Budgeting for permits, professional help, and compliance costs

One of the easiest ways to blow up a tiny-house budget is to treat the legal side like a last-minute fee instead of a real project cost. Permits, drawings, inspections, professional reviews, and compliance upgrades can add up fast, especially if you are trying to fit a unique design into a system that was built around standard houses. The money usually does not disappear in one giant payment. It leaks out in smaller charges: plan review fees, zoning applications, variance requests, septic evaluations, survey work, energy calculations, stamped drawings, reinspection fees, and the occasional "we need one more document" expense that shows up after you thought you were done.

A smart budget starts with the approval path, not the build price. If your tiny house is going on a foundation, you may need a building permit, site plan review, utility approvals, and possibly separate permits for electrical, plumbing, mechanical, grading, or septic work. If it is on wheels, the costs may shift toward zoning research, special-use applications, transport compliance, and whatever professional help you need to prove the unit fits the local rules. Either way, the legal path determines the cost structure. A project that looks cheaper on paper can become expensive if it requires multiple approvals or repeated revisions before anyone will sign off.

Permit fees themselves are often just the visible tip of the iceberg. A local permit might seem manageable, but the real budget pressure often comes from the documents needed to get that permit approved. Many tiny-house owners need a surveyor to verify setbacks or lot boundaries, a designer or draftsperson to prepare construction drawings, and sometimes an engineer to review structural details, foundation plans, roof loads, or alternative systems. If the house is unusual enough, the building department may want calculations or notes from a licensed professional before it will accept the plans. That is not necessarily overkill; it is the price of making a nonstandard project legible to a system that likes familiar paperwork.

It also helps to budget for the fact that tiny-house projects are more likely than standard builds to get revised. A conventional house plan may already fit the local code path. A tiny house often needs adjustments to satisfy ceiling height, loft access, egress, stair geometry, or occupancy rules. Every revision can mean more drafting time, more review time, and sometimes another round of fees. If you are working with a designer, builder, or consultant, ask how they handle revisions and whether the estimate includes one review cycle or several. A low upfront quote can turn into a much bigger bill if the first version of the plan does not pass muster.

Professional help is worth budgeting for even when you are trying to keep costs lean. The question is not whether you can do everything yourself. The question is which parts are too expensive to get wrong. A lawyer may be worth it if you are dealing with deed restrictions, a tricky zoning interpretation, a denial, or a property you are about to buy and cannot afford to misread. A planner or zoning consultant can be useful when the issue is land use and local procedure. An engineer or code-savvy designer is often the right call when the structure itself is the problem. Paying for the right expert early is usually cheaper than paying for the wrong assumption later.

That said, professional help should be targeted, not random. You do not need to hire a whole team just because the project feels intimidating. Start by identifying the bottleneck. If the question is whether the parcel can legally support the tiny house, a land-use professional may be the best first spend. If the question is whether the design can meet code, a building designer or engineer may save you from expensive redesign. If the issue is a dispute with the city or a private restriction on the deed, legal advice may matter more than another set of drawings. The best budget is the one that puts money where the risk actually is.

Compliance costs are the sneaky part, because they are not always labeled as "legal" even though they are driven by legal requirements. You may need a bigger septic system than you expected, upgraded electrical service, a driveway that meets access standards, fire separation materials, a foundation designed for frost depth, or a second exit that changes the whole layout. Sometimes the cheapest way to build the house is not the cheapest way to make it legal. If you are serious about living there long term, it is better to price in the compliance upgrades early than to discover halfway through the build that the project needs a major correction before occupancy.

A good rule is to keep a separate contingency fund for legal and compliance surprises, not just construction surprises. A lot of tiny-house owners budget for lumber, fixtures, and labor, then forget that approval delays can cost money too. You might pay for extra storage time, additional site visits, resubmittals, revised drawings, or temporary living arrangements while waiting on a permit. If your project depends on a deadline, build in room for slippage. Tiny-house legality has a way of turning "almost approved" into "still waiting" at the exact moment when you thought the hard part was over.

If you want a simple way to think about the budget, separate it into four buckets: getting informed, getting approved, getting built, and getting corrected. "Getting informed" includes research, consultations, and property review. "Getting approved" covers permits, applications, plan review, and inspections. "Getting built" is the actual construction work tied to code compliance. "Getting corrected" is the cushion for revisions, extra documentation, failed inspections, or site changes. That structure keeps you from pretending the legal side is free, and it helps you compare different tiny-house paths honestly. The cheapest-looking option is not always the cheapest once the rules show up.

When to hire a lawyer, planner, designer, or code consultant

There is a point in almost every tiny-house project where DIY stops being the smart move. The hard part is that you usually do not hit that point because something has gone terribly wrong. More often, you hit it because the project has become specific enough that a small mistake could cost you a permit, a lot of money, or the ability to live in the house at all. That is when bringing in the right professional starts looking less like an extra expense and more like damage control.

A lawyer is the person to call when the question is really about rights, restrictions, or risk. If you are dealing with a zoning denial, a confusing interpretation from the city, a deed restriction, a dispute with an HOA, or a permit appeal, legal advice can save you from guessing wrong. A lawyer is also useful if you are trying to structure ownership, lease land, negotiate with a landowner, or figure out whether a local rule is being applied correctly. If the issue could end up in a formal hearing, a written appeal, or a lawsuit, that is lawyer territory. Tiny-house law is full of places where the answer is not just "what do the rules say?" but "what can I do about it if the rules are being applied badly?"

A planner is different. A planner is usually the right person when you need help understanding how a piece of land fits into the local zoning system and how to move a project through that system without wasting time. If you are trying to figure out whether a parcel can support a second dwelling, whether an ADU path exists, whether a lot split is possible, or whether a variance is realistic, a planner can help translate the code into a usable strategy. That is especially helpful if you are early in the process and still trying to decide whether to buy land, apply for a permit, or redesign the project to fit the district. A good planner can often spot the land-use problems before you spend money on detailed plans that do not match local rules.

A designer, architect, or draftsperson becomes important when the project needs to be drawn in a way the permit office can actually use. Tiny-house plans are often clever, but "clever" is not the same thing as permit-ready. If your structure has lofts, unusual stairs, multi-use spaces, off-grid systems, or a tight footprint that pushes against code requirements, a designer can turn the idea into documents that speak the language of the building department. This matters most when your project is not a standard kit house or a simple rectangle on a slab. If you need site plans, elevations, sections, foundation details, or a layout that shows egress and clearances clearly, professional drawings can prevent a lot of back-and-forth.

A code consultant is the specialist to call when the main problem is technical compliance. That might sound similar to what a designer does, but the focus is different. A code consultant lives in the details of what the code requires and how officials are likely to read it. If you are trying to fit a tiny house into a narrow code category, interpret loft rules, satisfy stair or ladder issues, work through a manufactured-housing or RV-style classification, or answer a reviewer's objections line by line, a code consultant can be a lifesaver. This is the person you want when you already know the general path, but you need help proving that the design meets the applicable standards.

The biggest mistake people make is hiring too late. They wait until the permit is denied, the structure is built, or the land is already purchased, and then they ask a professional to fix a problem that was visible from the start. That can still be worth doing, but it is much more expensive and much less flexible than getting help earlier. If you are spending more than you can afford to lose on land, drawings, fabrication, or site work, that is a clue that a professional review may be cheaper than a bad assumption. The same is true if your project depends on one narrow approval, one exception, or one official's interpretation. The less room you have for error, the more valuable expert help becomes.

You do not need a full team for every tiny house. In fact, hiring everyone at once can be overkill. A better approach is to match the professional to the problem. If the issue is "Can I do this on this lot?" start with zoning or planning help. If the issue is "Will the building department accept this design?" start with a designer or code consultant. If the issue is "What are my legal rights if the city says no?" talk to a lawyer. If the issue is "How do I make the plan clear enough to submit?" bring in design support. The right question usually points to the right person.

A few warning signs mean you should stop improvising and get professional help fast: you are receiving contradictory answers from different departments; the project depends on a variance, appeal, or special permit; the property has deed restrictions or an HOA; the structure is being classified in a gray area; or the build involves alternative systems that local officials may not be familiar with. In those situations, a small upfront fee can prevent a very expensive wrong turn. Tiny-house projects are full of people who are perfectly capable of building a home, but not necessarily of navigating every legal and technical issue alone. Knowing when to hand off part of the job is part of building legally, too.

A practical roadmap from dream to legal move-in

The cleanest way to move a tiny house from "idea" to "I can actually sleep here tonight" is to treat the project like a sequence of legal gates, not one giant approval. Each gate has its own question. First: can this structure legally exist in the category you want? Second: can it go on the parcel you picked? Third: can it be built, connected, and occupied under the rules that apply there? If you skip a gate, the later ones do not magically fix the earlier problem. A beautiful set of plans does not rescue a bad zoning fit, and a friendly zoning answer does not replace the need for code-compliant drawings.

Start with the property, not the house. Before you spend money on a builder, a trailer, or custom drawings, confirm the zoning district, the minimum lot requirements, the allowed dwelling types, and any overlays or private restrictions that could change the answer. Then ask the practical question that matters most: what specific legal path does this parcel support? In some places that will be a foundation-built dwelling. In others it might be an accessory dwelling unit, a manufactured home, or a tiny house on wheels used in a limited way. If the parcel cannot support the path you want, that is not a paperwork problem. It is a strategy problem.

Once the parcel looks promising, match the structure to the legal category as early as possible. This is where a lot of tiny-house plans go sideways. People design the home they want first and only later discover that the local government does not recognize that design as a dwelling, or only recognizes it if it is built a certain way. If your path requires a permanent foundation, design for that from day one. If it requires residential code compliance, do not assume RV-style compromises will slide. If the project depends on being treated as an accessory unit, make sure the lot already has a primary residence and that the local rules actually allow a second home there. The legal category is not a label you slap on at the end; it shapes the build from the beginning.

After that, build your permit plan around the exact approvals the project needs. For some tiny houses, that means zoning confirmation first, then building permit, then utility approvals, then inspections, then occupancy. For others, it may include a variance, a special-use permit, a septic review, or a driveway permit before the building department will even look at the structure. The order matters because one approval often depends on another. A permit office may not review construction drawings until zoning says the use is allowed. A utility provider may not set a meter until the site plan is approved. A health department may not sign off on septic until the dwelling count and location are settled. The fastest path is usually the one where you know which office needs to speak first.

Keep your documents aligned. Tiny-house projects get delayed when the zoning application says one thing, the site plan says another, and the construction drawings suggest a third version of the project. If you tell one office it is a permanent residence and another office it is an RV-style unit, you are creating a problem even if you did not mean to. Every document should tell the same story about use, size, location, utilities, and occupancy. That does not mean you hide anything. It means you stop accidentally giving the government three different projects and asking it to approve all of them at once. Consistency is one of the most underrated legal tools you have.

It also helps to budget for the boring parts early. A lot of tiny-house owners plan for lumber, appliances, and finishes, then act shocked when the legal side adds cost. But permits, surveys, engineered drawings, septic work, utility upgrades, driveway access, and professional consultations are not optional decorations. They are often the price of making the project real. If your budget only works when every approval is free, instant, and simple, the plan is too thin. A better budget includes a cushion for revisions, resubmittals, and the possibility that the first legal path you choose will not be the one that works.

As you move through the process, keep a running file of every answer you get in writing. Save emails, permit notes, plan review comments, zoning confirmations, and any letters that describe what is allowed. Tiny-house projects often depend on small distinctions, and those distinctions are easy to forget when time passes or staff changes. Written records protect you from the classic "that is not what we said" problem. They also help when you need to show a lender, insurer, contractor, or future buyer that the home was approved through the proper channels. If an official gives you a verbal answer that matters, follow up politely and ask for confirmation by email.

Finally, be willing to change course before the project gets expensive. A legal strategy is not a promise to make one exact design work at all costs. It is a way to find the path that can actually survive the rules in front of you. Sometimes that means shrinking the plan, changing the structure type, moving to a different parcel, or waiting for a permit path to open up. That is not failure. That is what smart tiny-house planning looks like. The goal is not just to build something small. The goal is to end up in a home you can occupy without wondering whether the next letter from the city will tell you to leave.

Conclusion

By the time you get to this point, the legal side of tiny living should feel less mysterious and more like a set of moving parts you can actually sort through. That is the real win. Tiny-house law is rarely about finding one magic rule that solves everything. It is about matching the right structure to the right property, the right approvals to the right jurisdiction, and the right expectations to the way the place will actually be used.

If there is one habit that makes the biggest difference, it is slowing down before you spend money. Not forever. Just long enough to confirm the category, the parcel, and the approval path. A lot of people start with the build because that part is exciting. But the build is only one piece of the puzzle. A tiny house can be beautifully designed, carefully constructed, and still run into trouble if the lot does not allow it, the code path does not fit it, or the paperwork never gets lined up in the first place.

The good news is that tiny-house legality is usually more navigable than it first appears once you stop treating it like a single yes-or-no question. Most projects become manageable when you break them into smaller questions: What is this structure legally considered? Where is it allowed to go? What standards does it have to meet? Who has to approve it? What proof do they want? Those questions are not glamorous, but they are the ones that keep projects alive.

That also means you do not have to know every rule in every place. You only need to know how to find the rules that control your project and how to read them without guessing. In practice, that means checking the exact property, getting answers in writing when possible, and paying attention to the difference between what someone thinks is allowed and what the code actually says. Tiny-house projects get a lot easier when you stop relying on rumor, internet folklore, or someone else's success story in another county.

It is also worth remembering that "legal" is not always the same as "easy," and "hard" is not always the same as "impossible." Some paths take more paperwork, more patience, or more professional help than you expected. That does not mean the project is dead. It usually means the project needs a better strategy. Sometimes the smartest move is to adjust the design. Sometimes it is to change the legal category. Sometimes it is to choose a different parcel or a different town. Flexibility is not giving up; it is how people actually get from idea to move-in.

And if the process has felt frustrating, that is normal too. Tiny-house rules can be clunky, inconsistent, and annoyingly local. But they are still rules, which means they can be learned, tested, and worked with. Once you understand who controls what, what each office cares about, and which details matter most, the whole process stops feeling like a wall and starts feeling like a map.

The point is not to become obsessed with legal trivia. The point is to protect your time, your money, and your ability to live in the home you are building. If you keep that goal in view, the paperwork, the questions, and the approvals start to make more sense. Tiny living can be simple. The path to getting there usually is not. But it is a path you can follow on purpose.

That is the mindset to carry forward: stay curious, stay specific, and keep checking the facts that actually control your project. Tiny-house success is rarely about luck. It is usually about doing the boring legal work early enough that the fun part has a place to land.

Appendix: Tiny House Legal Tools and Resources

Once you start dealing with tiny-house rules in the real world, the hardest part is often not the law itself but keeping track of what matters, who said it, and where you found it. A good paper trail can save you from bad assumptions, wasted money, and the classic "someone told me it was fine" problem. That is what this appendix is for: a place to gather the tools that help you stay organized, ask better questions, and speak the same language as planners, building officials, and code reviewers. Instead of improvising every time a new issue comes up, you can lean on a few simple reference points that make the process less chaotic and a lot more manageable. Use the materials that follow as working tools, not decoration, and keep them close whenever you are researching a property, preparing an application, or trying to get a straight answer from a local office.

Tiny house research checklist

Before you spend real money on a tiny house project, do a hard reality check on the property, the structure, and the approval path. The goal is not to collect every possible detail. The goal is to find the few facts that decide whether the project is legal, fixable, or dead on arrival. If you can answer those facts early, you save yourself from the classic tiny-house trap: building something beautiful that the local rules have no interest in welcoming.

Start with the land. What is the parcel zoned for, and what uses are actually allowed there? Do not stop at the broad label like residential, rural, or agricultural. Look for the specific limits that matter to tiny houses: minimum lot size, minimum dwelling size, whether more than one dwelling is allowed, whether accessory dwelling units are permitted, and whether the property sits in an overlay district or special zone with extra rules. If the land is in an HOA or covered by deed restrictions, check those too. A tiny house can be perfectly fine under public zoning and still get blocked by private covenants.

Next, figure out what kind of structure you are dealing with in the eyes of the law. Is it on wheels, on a foundation, or something in between? Is it meant to be a permanent home, a guest unit, an accessory dwelling, or a movable recreational unit? That classification matters because it often determines which department gets involved first and which code path applies. A tiny house on wheels may look like a home, but the local government may treat it like a trailer or RV. A foundation-built tiny house may be treated like any other dwelling, which can be good or bad depending on the lot and the code requirements.

Then check the site itself. Can the parcel actually support daily living without improvising around the rules? Ask about water, sewer or septic, power, road access, and emergency access. If the property needs a septic system, find out whether there is a site approved for it and whether the lot can handle the required setbacks. If it needs a well or utility hookup, confirm that those services are available and legal to connect. A lot of tiny-house projects fail not because the house is too small, but because the site cannot support a legal dwelling at all.

It also helps to know what approvals are required before anyone starts building or placing the home. Some projects need zoning approval first, then building permits, then utility approvals, then inspections. Others need a variance, special-use permit, or accessory dwelling approval just to get off the ground. If you are planning to live in the unit full-time, ask whether occupancy is allowed and under what conditions. If you are hoping to use it temporarily while building a larger home, ask whether the jurisdiction allows temporary occupancy and what time limits apply. "We'll figure it out later" is how expensive mistakes happen.

Here is a simple checklist you can use before you commit:

Property: exact address, parcel number, and jurisdiction

Zoning: district, allowed uses, minimum lot size, minimum dwelling size, and ADU rules

Private restrictions: HOA rules, deed restrictions, easements, or recorded covenants

Structure type: wheels, foundation, modular, manufactured, or other

Use: full-time residence, ADU, guest house, temporary housing, or rental

Utilities: water, sewer or septic, electricity, propane, and internet if needed

Access: road frontage, driveway, emergency access, and delivery access

Permits: zoning approval, building permit, septic permit, electrical permit, and occupancy approval

Code path: which building code or housing standard applies

Written confirmation: names, dates, and copies of any official answers

As you work through that list, pay attention to the places where people tend to assume instead of verify. Do not assume the parcel is legal just because it is vacant. Do not assume a tiny house on wheels is automatically easier because it is movable. Do not assume a county rule overrides a city rule, or that a city rule overrides a private restriction. And do not assume one official's casual comment is the same thing as an approved interpretation. Tiny-house legality lives in details, and the details are usually what separate a workable plan from a costly guess.

One of the smartest things you can do is build your checklist around the question, "What could stop this project?" not "What sounds nice to know?" That means your first calls and emails should focus on the deal-breakers: zoning, use, structure type, and site constraints. Once those are clear, you can move on to design choices, finishes, and comfort features. If you reverse that order, you risk falling in love with a layout before you know whether the law will ever let it exist where you want it.

Keep the checklist with your notes, maps, screenshots, emails, and permit documents. Tiny-house projects get messy fast, and a clean record is worth more than a good memory. If someone later says, "We never told you that," you will want to be able to point to the date, the person, and the exact answer. That paper trail is not just for protection. It is how you turn a vague tiny-house idea into a project you can actually defend.

Questions to ask your local planning department

When you finally sit down with the local planning department, the goal is not to launch into a speech about tiny houses in general. The goal is to figure out what this office actually cares about for your parcel. That means asking narrow, factual questions that force a useful answer. Start with the basics: What is the zoning designation for the property? How many dwelling units are allowed on the lot? Is a tiny house treated differently if it is on wheels, on a foundation, or used as an accessory dwelling unit? Those three questions alone can reveal whether you are dealing with a real path forward or a polite dead end.

It also helps to ask how the department defines the structure you want to build or place. Some offices care a lot about whether something is a dwelling, a recreational vehicle, a manufactured home, or an accessory structure. Others care more about use than labels. You want to know which category matters most in that jurisdiction, because the label can change the entire approval process. A good follow-up question is: If I submit plans for this kind of structure, what review process applies, and which department makes the final call? That keeps you from getting bounced between planning, building, and code enforcement with nobody taking ownership of the answer.

Another important line of questioning is about the site itself. Ask whether the parcel meets minimum lot size requirements, setback rules, frontage requirements, and access standards for the kind of dwelling you want. If the property is in a rural or unincorporated area, ask whether county rules differ from city rules and whether any overlays, floodplain limits, wildfire rules, or environmental restrictions apply. Planning staff often know these issues better than the average internet search suggests, and they can usually tell you pretty quickly if the land has a hidden problem that will matter later. If the project depends on a septic system, utility hookup, or driveway approval, ask which office handles that piece and whether planning has any land-use concerns before you spend money on engineering.

Do not forget private restrictions. Ask whether the property is subject to any recorded covenants, HOA rules, deed restrictions, or special district rules that could affect a tiny house. Planning departments do not always enforce private restrictions, but they can often tell you where to look or whether the area is known for them. If you are buying land, this question is worth asking early, because a parcel can be perfectly fine under public zoning and still be unusable because of private rules. You do not want to discover that after you have already ordered a build or signed a closing document.

It is also smart to ask about the exact path for getting a yes. If the project does not fit the standard rules, what options exist: administrative approval, variance, special-use permit, conditional use permit, accessory dwelling approval, or another local process? Ask what the office needs from you to review that path, how long it usually takes, and whether there are any common reasons applications get denied. If there is a form, ask for it. If there is a checklist, ask for it. If there is a staff member who handles tiny-house or ADU questions, ask to speak with that person. The more you can turn the conversation from theory into process, the more useful it becomes.

One of the best questions you can ask is also one of the simplest: "Can you tell me what would make this a clear yes, and what would make it a clear no?" That forces the office to move beyond vague caution and identify the actual deal-breakers. If they say the issue is unclear, ask what document, ordinance section, or code provision they would rely on. If they say they cannot give legal advice, ask for the rule they would use to evaluate the application. You are not trying to corner anyone. You are trying to get the logic out in the open so you can work with it instead of guessing.

Finally, ask how they want you to follow up. Should you send a written summary for confirmation? Can they respond by email? Is there a formal pre-application meeting? If you get a verbal answer, repeat it back in plain language and ask whether you understood it correctly. Then write down the date, name, title, and exact wording as soon as you can. Tiny-house projects often depend on small distinctions, and those distinctions are easy to lose if you rely on memory alone. The planning department does not have to do your whole project for you, but it should be able to tell you what rules are in play, what category your idea falls into, and what the next step is. Those are the questions that save time, money, and a whole lot of confusion later.

Glossary of zoning and building code terms

When tiny-house conversations get technical, the same few words keep showing up over and over. A lot of them sound familiar, but in zoning and building code land, familiar does not always mean simple. One office may use a term one way, another office may use it slightly differently, and a code section may attach a very specific meaning that is narrower than everyday speech. If you know the language, you can usually tell the difference between a real obstacle and a wording issue that just needs clarification.

Accessory dwelling unit, or ADU, means a secondary dwelling on the same lot as a primary home. It is usually smaller than the main house and may be attached, detached, or built into existing space like a garage conversion, depending on local rules. The key idea is that it is accessory to the main residence, not the primary use of the property. A tiny house may qualify as an ADU in one place and not in another, depending on size limits, owner-occupancy rules, and whether the local code allows detached units at all.

Setback is the required distance between a structure and a property line, street, or other boundary. Think of it as the code's way of making sure buildings do not crowd each other or sit too close to the edge of a lot. Tiny-house projects run into setbacks a lot because a smaller structure does not always mean a smaller site issue. A tiny house on a narrow parcel can still fail if the placement leaves too little room on the side, front, or rear. A setback is about location, not just size.

Lot coverage refers to how much of a parcel can be covered by buildings or other structures. A tiny house may be small enough to seem harmless, but if the lot already has a main house, garage, shed, driveway, and other improvements, the property may already be close to the maximum allowed coverage. Zoning codes use lot coverage to control density, drainage, and neighborhood character. It is one of those terms that can quietly matter a lot even when the house itself is tiny.

Dwelling unit means a place designed for people to live in, usually with sleeping, cooking, and sanitation facilities. This is one of the most important terms in the whole tiny-house world because zoning codes often regulate the number of dwelling units on a lot. If your tiny house counts as a separate dwelling unit, it may trigger rules about density, parking, setbacks, septic capacity, and minimum lot size. If it does not count as a dwelling unit, it may still be allowed as something else, like an accessory structure, but then it may not be legal for full-time occupancy.

Occupancy is about use, not just construction. A structure can be built safely and still be restricted in how it may be occupied. Some codes care whether a building is used for temporary stays, seasonal use, full-time residence, or guest accommodations. That is why a tiny house that looks identical on the outside can be treated very differently depending on whether someone plans to live there year-round, rent it out, or use it only part of the year. When officials ask about occupancy, they are usually trying to figure out which rules apply to the way the space will actually be used.

Variance is permission to deviate from a zoning rule in a specific case. It is not a general exemption and it is not a promise that every future tiny house can ignore the same rule. Usually, a variance requires showing that the property has a special hardship or unusual condition that makes strict compliance difficult. Conditional use permit and special use permit are related terms, but they work differently. Those permits usually allow a use the code already contemplates, as long as certain conditions are met. In plain English: a variance asks for relief from a rule, while a conditional or special use permit asks for approval to do something the code allows only in certain circumstances.

Certificate of occupancy, often shortened to CO or C of O, is the document that says a building may be legally occupied. In some places, it is issued after final inspections show the structure meets the applicable code and is safe for its intended use. For tiny houses, this term matters because a completed structure is not always ready to live in just because the construction is finished. If the local government requires a certificate of occupancy, you usually do not want to move in before you have it, even if the place looks done.

Foundation means the structural base that transfers a building's load to the ground. In tiny-house conversations, this word matters because a house on a permanent foundation is often treated very differently from a movable unit on wheels. A code official may ask whether the structure is on a slab, crawlspace, pier, or another approved system because that answer can determine whether the project is reviewed like a house, a temporary unit, or something else entirely. Permanent foundation usually signals that the structure is intended to stay put and be regulated as real property, not as a vehicle or trailer-based unit.

Egress means a safe way out. In building code language, it usually refers to emergency escape and rescue openings, exits, or paths that let people leave a structure quickly if there is a fire or other emergency. Tiny houses often get into trouble here because lofts, compact bedrooms, and narrow stairways can make the code uncomfortable unless the design clearly supports safe escape. Planned unit development, or PUD, is a zoning tool that allows a more flexible, negotiated layout than standard zoning. It can sometimes create room for tiny-house-friendly design, but it also comes with its own approval process and conditions.

Minimum square footage is exactly what it sounds like: the smallest size a dwelling must be under local rules. Not every jurisdiction uses this term, and some codes care more about room dimensions than total area, but when it appears, it can be a major barrier for tiny houses. A related term is habitable space, which means the parts of a dwelling intended for regular living, such as sleeping or living rooms. Storage, mechanical rooms, and some loft areas may not count the same way. That distinction matters because a tiny house can be "small" in total size while still meeting certain room requirements, or it can fail because the usable living space is too limited.

Recreational vehicle, or RV, and park model are terms that often come up when a tiny house is built on wheels. These categories usually fall under different standards than a conventional dwelling, and that difference can be helpful or limiting depending on your plan. An RV may be easier to move and may fit in places where a house would not, but it may also be restricted from full-time residential use. A park model is typically a larger recreational unit intended for seasonal or temporary occupancy, not a permanent home in the usual sense. The label matters because once a structure is classified as an RV-style unit, many local governments stop treating it like a standard house.

Suggested templates for permit and official correspondence

When you start asking for permission in writing, the quality of your paperwork matters almost as much as the answer you get back. A sloppy email can invite a vague reply. A clear one can save you weeks of back-and-forth. The goal is not to sound fancy. The goal is to make it easy for a planner, building official, or zoning staff member to understand exactly what you are asking, exactly which property you mean, and exactly what kind of tiny house project you are proposing. If you give them a clean fact pattern, you are more likely to get a clean response.

A good permit cover letter does three jobs at once: it identifies the property, describes the project, and points the reviewer to the specific approvals you are seeking. Keep it short enough that someone can read it quickly, but specific enough that they do not have to guess. Include the parcel address, parcel number if you have it, the zoning district, the structure type, and whether the tiny house will be on wheels, on a foundation, or used as an accessory dwelling unit. If you already know the utility plan, say so. If you know there is an existing house on the lot, say that too. The more your letter sounds like a real project and less like a general inquiry, the more useful the response will be.

Here is a simple template you can adapt for a permit submittal or pre-application packet:

Subject: Permit inquiry for [property address / parcel number]

Project description: I am proposing to place/build a [tiny house on wheels / foundation-built tiny house / accessory dwelling unit] at [address]. The structure will be approximately [square footage] and will be used as [primary residence / secondary dwelling / guest house / temporary housing].

Questions: Please confirm whether this use is allowed in the current zoning district, what permits are required, and whether any additional approvals, such as site plan review, variance, special use permit, or utility approvals, are needed.

Attachments: Site sketch, basic floor plan, parcel information, and any other supporting documents you would like me to provide.

Request: If possible, please respond in writing so I can make sure I understand the applicable requirements correctly.

That last line is important. You are not being difficult by asking for written confirmation. You are protecting yourself. Tiny-house projects get derailed all the time because someone remembers a phone conversation differently than the official who gave it. A written response gives you something concrete to refer back to if the project gets reviewed by a different person later. It also helps you avoid the classic problem where one department says "fine" and another department says "we never approved that."

If you need to ask a zoning question before filing an application, keep the message narrow. Do not ask, "Can I live tiny here?" That is too broad to answer well. Instead, ask something like: "Would a detached accessory dwelling unit of approximately 320 square feet be permitted on this parcel in the R-1 zoning district?" or "Does the code treat a tiny house on wheels as a dwelling, recreational unit, or something else for this property?" Specific questions get specific answers. Broad questions tend to get polite nonanswers.

When you are writing to an official, a respectful tone works better than a persuasive speech. You do not need to explain your whole life story or your philosophy about downsizing. You just need to show that you have done enough homework to make the question answerable. A simple opening like, "I'm researching a tiny-house project for the parcel listed below and want to make sure I understand the local requirements before I move forward," usually lands better than a dramatic pitch about sustainable living. The official is not there to be inspired. They are there to process information.

If you get a denial, delay, or confusing answer, your next message should focus on clarification, not argument. A good follow-up template might look like this:

Thank the official for the response.

Restate the specific issue you believe is blocking the project.

Ask whether the concern is zoning, building code, utilities, or a missing document.

Ask whether there is a path to address the issue, such as a revised plan, additional documentation, or a different permit type.

Request the relevant code section or policy reference if one applies.

That approach keeps the conversation moving. It also helps you separate real barriers from misunderstandings. Sometimes the first answer is not the final answer. Sometimes the office is reacting to incomplete information, or they are using a term differently than you are. A calm request for the rule in writing can expose that quickly.

For more formal situations, such as a variance request, appeal, or special-use permit, your correspondence should read like a project summary rather than a casual email. State who you are, what you are asking for, where the property is, and why the request is needed. Then explain the facts that support it without overselling. If the parcel is unusually shaped, if the lot already contains another dwelling, if the proposed tiny house will improve housing access without creating a safety issue, those are the kinds of facts that belong in the letter. Keep the language plain. Officials are much more likely to trust a clear, grounded request than a dramatic one.

If you want a simple all-purpose email template for initial contact, this version works well:

Hello, I'm planning a tiny-house project for [property address / parcel number] and want to make sure I understand the local requirements before I submit anything. The project is a [tiny house on wheels / foundation-built tiny house / ADU] of approximately [square footage], intended for [use]. Could you let me know which office should review this, what permits or approvals may be required, and whether there are any zoning or code issues I should address first? If possible, I would appreciate a written response. Thank you for your time.

You do not need a perfect template to get started. You just need one that is specific, polite, and easy to answer. In tiny-house work, that alone can put you miles ahead of the people who show up with a dream and no paper trail.

www.ingramcontent.com/pod-product-compliance
Lightning Source LLC
LaVergne TN
LVHW100319210926
848480LV00003B/1186
* 9 7 8 1 9 2 3 4 5 2 1 3 8 *